The Last Rebels

Roger Huff

Parson's Porch Books

The Last Rebels
ISBN: Softcover
Copyright © 2024 by Roger Huff

Parson's Porch Books is an imprint of Parson's Porch & Company (PP&C) in Cleveland, Tennessee. PP&C is a self-funded charity which earns money by publishing books of noted authors, representing all genres. Its face and voice is **David Russell Tullock** who you can contact at: dtullock@parsonsporch.com.

Parson's Porch & Company *turns books into bread & milk* by sharing its profits with the poor.

www.parsonsporch.com

The Last Rebels

Chapter 1—Escape

Way March dashed toward the ten-foot tall brick wall. The baby he carried laughed and squealed like they played a game. The bullets flying around them said different.

"Stop! Stop! In the name of The Group, stop!"

More bullets zinged around the baby and Way.

Way didn't look back. Didn't stop. He eyed the open gate. The refuse truck was through the opening and the gate would close in a few seconds. If he didn't make it through, it was over.

He heard a Corpsman that must have been a couple of hundred feet away. "Stop!"

The gate started closing. Way heard the Corpsman gain. Bullets hit all around. The baby laughed.

Way didn't know if he would make it. The gate seemed to move faster than ever, and his legs were not used to the run. He stumbled but managed to stay upright.

He looked to the closing gate, then to the shrinking opening. Back to the gate. Back to the opening. He had several feet to run, and the gate just had a few feet until it closed for the night.

"Stop!" Another Corpsman gained on Way from behind.

Way made it to the opening and squeezed through. The gate caught his foot. Way jerked and managed to get free and keep from losing his house slipper.

He heard the two Corpsmen reach the gate. He held the baby tight and kept running. He knew the Corpsmen would have to get approval from their superiors to open the gate. No one left the walled city without permission from the authorities, not even the Corpsmen. Way figured he had about fifteen minutes to put some distance between himself and however many Corpsmen gave chase.

Way went into the woods. For the first time in his life he was outside the city's walls. Where to go?

The chip.

He had to do something about the chip. With it in the back of his hand it didn't matter where he went or how well he hid. Corpsmen would find him in a matter of minutes once they dialed in on the chip.

The chip gave The Group his location at all times. It told when he slept and contained his medical records, education records, and purpose history. It held all the information there was to know about him. The only thing it didn't know was his thoughts, and The Group was working to take care of that.

He sat by a tree and held the baby on his lap. He had a hard time slowing his breathing.

The moon was not out.

Way looked at the place where the chip had been injected on his first birthday. Most days he didn't even think of it. It was just an ever-present lump.

Workers for The Group, well, everyone worked for The Group, had probably already zeroed in on his coordinates. He had maybe ten minutes before Corpsmen arrived.

He dug at his skin. He dug harder and harder. He bled. Eventually, he got to the chip and pulled it out. He flung it into the darkness.

Thankfully, he didn't have to worry about the baby having a chip. His Injection Day was set for the next day, his first birthday. He was to get his chip and his name. That is, if his mother, Way's domestic partner, decided she wanted to keep him. And that was why Way was in his predicament.

Many years before, The Group had ordained that when an offspring was born into a domestic partnership, the mother had one year to decide if she wanted to keep the offspring or wanted it extinguished with the final decision coming on the offspring's Injection Day. That was why the offspring didn't have a chip yet. The Group did not want to put out the resources of chipping an offspring that was going to be extinguished. And an offspring did not receive his name unless the mother decided she wanted to keep him. The Group felt there was no need to name an offspring that was to be extinguished.

Minutes earlier, Way and Luka, his domestic partner, sat in the front room of their pod.

Way waved. "You're having him extinguished?"

Luka wouldn't look Way's direction. "You heard me."

"How can you do that?" Way motioned toward the baby playing on the floor. "Look at him. He's a happy boy. He's not any problem."

Luka scoffed. "Maybe not for you. From the time I pick him up from Groupcare at seven until I take him back the next morning is the worst part of my day. No, my life."

"But—"

"No, no buts. You deal with him three hours a night and maybe a couple of times through the night. I pick him up from Groupcare and take him back. I get up with him when you don't. He's just not worth it."

"I'll pick him up from Groupcare every night," Way said. "I'll take him back every morning. You won't have to worry with him. I'll bathe him and put him to bed. I'll get up with him through the night all the time."

Luka rolled her eyes. "Don't beg. It's unbecoming. You know The Group sees offspring as a negative when it comes to gaining authority at my purpose. It will be best for me if I don't have him holding me back."

"What about me?" Way leaned back on the gray couch and looked to the gray ceiling. "I want him. I love him."

"Love him?" Luka flared a nostril. "Why would you love him? To say he's a nuisance wouldn't begin to tell the half of it."

Way rose from the couch, took a step, scooped the baby up and hugged him. "Why wouldn't I love him. He's the best thing that ever happened to me."

The baby smiled and patted Way's back.

Luka folded her legs in front of her with her feet resting on the edge of the couch. She wrapped her arms around her legs. "Charming."

Way closed his eyes and held the baby closer. "Mmmm. I love you, little offspring."

"Oh, please."

"Here, take him." Way held the baby down toward Luka.

Luka pushed the baby back toward Way. "No. I don't want to hold him. I've had enough of him to last a lifetime. I really don't know if I can take one more night in the same pod with him. Tomorrow morning when I take him to the Extinguishing Center can not come soon enough."

"Don't I have a say?" Way rocked the baby from side to side. "I am the father, you know."

"And you know that makes no difference. I'm the mother, and I say he gets extinguished. The Group says the mother has the choice. He came from my body. My body, my choice."

"But he's been out of your body a year. He's a completely separate being."

"That's not the way The Group sees it." Luka raised a shoulder and tilted her head. "And I like the way The Group sees it."

Way knew his face was reddening, and if he hadn't been holding the baby, he would have been gesturing wildly. Just as he started to launch into a tirade about The Group's law, he caught a glimpse of one of the video cameras that hung just beneath the ceiling in each corner of the room.

The cameras. Way knew that everything in their pod was videoed. Everything. Way wondered if he had already said enough to warrant a visit from a Corpsman.

Luka noted Way looking at the camera. "Yes, you might want to be careful."

Way put the baby back on the floor and sat next to Luka. He gripped her knee. "Can we talk about this? Is there any way I can get you to keep him? I mean, look at him. He's so tiny and helpless. We're young. Maybe you'll get used to him. I had hoped we could have more."

Luka's jaw dropped. "More? You must be kidding. Do you think I'm going to have my monthly entitlements decreased so we can have another offspring taking up space in the world? Eating food that could go to someone else? Breathing oxygen that could go to someone else? You seem to have a hard time remembering The Group's decrees."

"I know." Way slouched back. "With every offspring a couple has, their individual monthly entitlement is decreased. Less food, I get it. People are penalized for having offspring."

Luka glared at Way and pointed at the camera. "Need I remind you? The Group has access to everything you say and do. I've made up my mind."

"What if you change your mind? We've only been together three years. What if someday you wish we still had him?"

"Not quite three years," Luka said as she raised her finger. "The three years is three days away." She inhaled. "And that conveniently brings me to something else I need to tell you since we're talking about these things that bring you such distress anyway."

Way's shoulders slumped.

"Our partnership is up for renewal in three days, and I have no intention of renewing."

"But—"

"Don't whine. The Group says both partners have to agree to stay in the partnership. If either wants out, they get out, no questions asked. They just walk away. I'm walking away. And as far as extinguishing him," she pointed at the baby, "you know it's the mother's choice. And my choice is to extinguish him. He's too much of an inconvenience."

"Why don't you want to renew the partnership?"

For the first time that evening, Luka smiled. She twirled a strand of her brown hair around her finger. "I've found someone else. Someone I want to be with."

Way's chest rose and fell. "Who is it? Where did you meet?"

Luka continued to smile and twirl the hair around her finger. "We work together."

The knots in his stomach formed so fast, Way thought he was going to vomit. He blinked. "You're ending our partnership so you can be with someone else?"

"Well, I'm not ending it so I can be with someone else. I was going to end it anyway. It just happens that I found him and we hit it off fabulously. As soon as your and my partnership is dissolved, he and I will sign the paperwork to begin our partnership. Everything else is taken care of. We received approval from all the proper sources. All we have to do is sign."

"Do I know him? Do you love him?"

"You don't know him." Luka sneered. "He wouldn't associate with the likes of you." She drifted back to her dreamy expression. "Partnering with him is going to be so good for me. He's connected with all the right people. He'll help me advance in my purpose. We're so excited. We both think we can make a long-term commitment. Why, I can see our relationship lasting six or nine years."

"But—"

"No. There you go again," Luka said. "Again, I've made the decisions about our partnership and the offspring." She poked her thumb toward the camera. "And you need to be careful. You've already pushed it to the limit. I'm surprised Corpsmen haven't come knocking and dragged you away. I think you've already done more than enough to warrant it. In fact, if you give me any more grief over either decision, I may call them myself and turn you in."

The digital clock on the wall buzzed. The evening had gotten away from Way. In just fifteen minutes, at 10 p.m., the pod's lights would dim. Way didn't feel like going to bed, but it was another of The Group's regulations. Lights were dimmed, all electronics turned off, and all day-working world citizens had to be in bed at 10 p.m. The nightly recording, known as the Grand Matron's Encouragement, would start. Many times, the Grand Matron's Encouragement kept Way from getting a good night's sleep as it played until 6 a.m. when the morning alarms went off, lights brightened and day-working world citizens prepared for their purpose.

The Grand Matron's Encouragement was a recording of Grand Matron Filleen Tannon speaking to world citizens to, in her words, "Strengthen their faith and trust in The Group."

Way had memorized the Encouragement: "I serve The Group. The Group knows best. The Group has my best interests in mind. It is all about The Group. I am nothing without The Group. The Group takes care of me. The Group loves me. The Group is all I need. The Group has all I need." And on and on.

Luka stood and left the room. Way knew she was preparing for bed. His mind raced. He had less than fifteen minutes. Fifteen minutes and he had to go to bed. The next morning Luka would take the offspring to the Extinguishing Center.

Way went to the door, but didn't know why. He knew it was locked. Doors and windows always locked at 7 p.m.

The baby played on the floor.

Way heard the shower running.

One idea.

He picked up the one gray chair in the room and went to the window. He had to get a good hit. Corpsmen would arrive in a matter of minutes after the first time the chair struck the window.

Way took the metal frame chair by the legs and swung with all he had. Nothing. He knew the pod's security system had alerted Corpsmen.

He swung again. Small cracks spider-webbed in the middle of the window. With his fingers hurting, Way adjusted his grip on the chair legs. He had the baby's attention, but was thankful the shower was running and he did not have Luka's.

Another swing, and the spider web grew. Another and another. Finally he broke through.

Way ran to the baby, scooped him up and went back to the window. He cleared glass from the frame. Lifting first one leg and then the other over the window frame. He stood on the ledge of the second-story pod and held the baby tight.

Across the way the gate opened for one of its few times of the day to allow the refuse trucks to take away the city's leftover food and other rubbish.

There was Way's chance.

Up the street, a light bobbed and grew closer. Way believed it was from a Corpsman's flashlight: a Corpsman running to Way's pod.

Way took a deep breath. He heard a scanning card run through the lock outside the door. Another Corpsman already on the scene.

Way jumped. He hit the ground and went into a roll, still clutching the baby. Way got to his feet and raced toward the gate.

"Stop! Stop in the name of The Group!" yelled a Corpsman from the direction of the broken window.

Chapter 2—Found

In the woods, Way tried to calm his breathing. He needed to sit a minute. Just a minute. He thought he could afford it. Even though Corpsmen were surely already in the woods, he believed it would help him.

Way sat with his back to a tree. He still held the baby. Leaning his head against the tree, Way closed his eyes. He couldn't stay long.

Someone covered Way's mouth. A dark figure came from the other side and grabbed the baby from Way.

"Come on! Come on!"

While covering Way's mouth, the person wrapped an arm around his chest and dragged him. "We've got to get them out of here!"

"I know. I know," said the person carrying the baby.

For several minutes, they moved Way and the baby deeper in the woods. They came to a cave. As soon as they were in, several people in the cave moved to cover the opening.

Finally, Way's mouth was uncovered.

Way got free and took quick stock of the little bit he could see in the cave. "Who are you? What are you doing with us?"

With a gesture of surrender, the man who covered Way's mouth smiled. His shoulder-length hair hung in curls. "Whoa, brother. Just a minute. We want to help you all. I'm Peter. Jesus Christ is King of kings and Lord of lords."

The man who carried the baby stepped beside Way. He stood at least six inches taller than Way. "You might want to calm yourself, bud. For better or worse and at great risk to ourselves, we're saving you and this baby's lives."

Men, women, and children gathered around Way.

One of the women took the baby from the man who had carried him. "Isn't he a doll." She smiled, cooed, and put a finger to the baby's chin.

More women, and girls, teenage and younger, stepped to the woman holding the baby. They fussed over him. The baby squealed and waved.

Way relaxed.

Peter gripped Way's shoulder. "It's all right, brother. You're among friends. We're going to do everything we can to help you and that little fellow."

"But, Peter, how much help can we really give?" asked the tall man who had carried the baby. "We got our people to think of. These two'll be an extra burden, as if we don't have enough already."

Lowering his gaze, Peter rubbed his beard. "Now, Abe, this isn't the time to talk about it. I mean, he's standing right in front of you."

Abe spoke through gritted teeth. "I don't care where he's standing. We need to talk about it, and he needs to know what it costs us to have him and that kid around."

Way looked from Peter to Abe and back. "I appreciate that you got me out of the woods and away from the Corpsmen, but I'm not asking for anything. The offspring and I can go."

"I'll hear of no such thing!" An older woman with gray-streaked hair stepped out from among those around the baby. "These two need our help, and Abe, I'm ashamed you would even suggest otherwise."

"But, Mom," Abe said.

"No buts about it, boy." The woman held a shaky, scraggly finger inches from Abe's nose. "Your daddy never turned anyone away, and as long as I'm around you won't either. One of these days, if those thugs get me or I pass on another way, you can do what you want, but as long as I'm here, we're taking care of everyone we possibly can." Mom's features softened, and she turned to Way. "Please excuse my boy. I don't know why he has such a lack of compassion."

Abe's shoulders rounded. He slunk to the back of the cave.

Speechless bordering on shock, Way felt a reverence for Mom.

Peter tried, with little success, to hide a grin. Finally, the grin disappeared. "Don't you worry, Mom. This man and his boy will be safe with us. Nobody's going to throw them to the wolves."

Mom nodded. "Well, just see there's no more such talk. These two have obviously had a rough night. We need to do what we can to ease their minds." She smiled and motioned toward the baby. "He seems to be enjoying his little adventure and all the attention he's getting." She motioned back to Way. "This one here, he could probably use a little mind-easing."

"He could use some shoes, too." Peter noted Way's slippers. "We can probably round up something more appropriate for living out here in the woods. What size do you wear?"

"Size?"

"Yeah, size. What size do you wear?"

Way glanced from one person to the next. They all seemed to take an unusual interest in the answer he wasn't able to provide. "I'm sorry. I don't know what you're talking about."

"See? Man can't even tell you his shoe size, and you think he won't be a hindrance to us?" Abe called from the back of the cave.

"Boy, cool it!" Mom yelled back at him.

Peter took a few seconds to hide another grin. After he regained his composure, he spoke gently to Way. "You see, brother, shoes come in sizes. They can be eight, eight-and-a-half, nine, nine-and-a-half and so on. The longer your foot the bigger the number."

"Okay." Way offered a slow nod. "I've never heard of that. I don't have any idea what size I wear. All I know is that every year The Group brings me two new pairs. It also gives me clothes: seven gray shirts and seven gray pairs of pants for the year."

"All gray?" Peter wrinkled his nose.

"Why, yes."

"Because that Group can't allow anyone to be their own individual."

"The Group just doesn't want anyone to be above anyone else. It wants us to all be on the same level. No one better, no one worse. The Group gives us everything we need. The Group gives us our food daily, some items weekly, some items monthly and some items yearly."

"You know he's brainwashed, don't you?" Abe called from the back of the cave.

"Hush, boy!" Mom called back. "Let Brother Peter talk to the man."

Peter crossed his arms. "Everyone gets the same? The cleaning lady gets the same as the doctor?"

Way furrowed his brow. "Of course! The Group says it wouldn't be fair otherwise. The Group says no one person is better than any other. We're all equal. We just have different purposes."

"You sound like you approve."

Way scoffed. "Of course. That's exactly as it should be, all equal. The Group knows best."

"Who says?"

Way looked to the cave ceiling. "The Group does, I guess."

Peter poked a thumb toward the baby. "And what about him? Does that Group know best for him?"

Way curled his lip. "Yes."

"What were you and the baby doing in the woods? It seems that would be a pretty stiff penalty."

"It is." Way covered his mouth. "It's the death penalty."

Way told those gathered how Luka planned to have the baby extinguished the next day, that he had grown to love the boy, and didn't want to see that happen to him. He told them about his spur of the moment decision to escape with the boy.

"All he got was a peck of trouble for hisself and us," Abe called.

Mom grabbed a wooden spoon from a nearby pot and raised it. "Boy, if I hear one more peep out of you, I'm going to turn you over my knee, and thrash you with this here spoon. I don't care how big or how old you are."

Another man stepped out from among the crowd. "Peter, you think it's about time to get him and the boy settled for the night?"

"Probably so, Antin. Can you fix him a pallet? I'd say it's time for all of us to get settled."

"That's dangerous." It was Abe from the back. "We don't know this man. What if he leads the KGB right to us?"

Way furrowed his brow. "The what? What is he talking about?"

Antin laughed and clapped. He looked toward the back of the cave. "Abe, if you had seen his face just now, I believe you'd know there's no worries. No way he's a good enough actor to pull off a look like that."

"What is the KGB? Why would I lead it to you?"

Peter pressed his palms together. "In a nutshell, the KGB was the government police in the old Soviet Union before it broke up."

Way scratched his head. "I still don't understand. What's the Soviet Union?"

"Oh, my goodness!" Abe's frustration was clear.

Peter massaged his ear lobe between his thumb and index finger. "It's clear that Group bunch succeeded in wiping out basic history. What do you know, brother?"

"Why do you call me brother? We're not brothers. I've never seen you, any of you, in my life."

"You're a believer, aren't you? A Christian?"

"A Christian? Now, there's a term I'm familiar with, but I'm not a Christian."

"But you ran away with the boy." Peter shifted his weight from one foot to the other. "I figured you to be a Christian since you didn't want the baby killed and you escaped the city."

"No." Way wrinkled his nose. "I'm no Christian. Not that I have a problem with Christians. The Group says being a Christian is fine as long as you don't try to push it off on someone else. What one person believes is no more or less valid than what another person believes. 'To each his own,' The Group says."

"But, the baby …," Antin started the sentence, but didn't go anywhere with it.

Way tilted his head to one side. "It has nothing to do with being a Christian. I knew his day was coming, but I guess it made it more real when my partner said she was going to have him extinguished tomorrow. Even though I knew I shouldn't, at least not until after his naming and chip injection, I got attached to him. When she said she was going to take him to the Extinguishing Center, something came over me, and I just couldn't let that happen."

Mom shook that shaky, scraggly finger, but it came with a smile. "Christian or not, it was God that put it in you to save that baby."

"With all due respect, madam, I don't hold your belief against you, but I don't believe in any of the gods. The Group doesn't mind people believing in a god. It just doesn't want anyone pushing their beliefs on, or judging, anyone else." Way stopped a moment. He stroked his chin. "In fact, your group doesn't seem to be like the Christians we have in the city. You're more like the rebels that we see executed every week—" he stopped himself.

"Don't worry, brother, er, sir, you didn't tell us anything we didn't already figure," Peter said. "I'd like to hear about those Christians that are all right in your Group's eyes."

Way went tight-lipped, and his eyes darted from side to side.

"Go ahead." Peter motioned. "We won't hurt you. You're in as safe a place as you can be."

"Yes, you are, sonny. Yes, you are." It seemed that Mom loved to shake that finger. That time in a reassuring manner.

Way drew a deep breath and exhaled. "All right. The Christians in my city and in the rest of the World Community are free to worship as they please. They believe all religions lead to the same place. And they oppose anyone who believes that that Jesus man is the only way to get there."

Peter went to a cave wall, picked something up and held it out to Way. "How about this?"

It was a book. The cover's edges were frayed and torn all around; the page edges well-worn. In the dim firelight of the cave, Way saw "Holy Bible" on the cover. "I've seen these before. I assume that is a version that was printed before The Group came into power. It would have been destroyed years ago in the city."

No one in the cave said a word, but Way thought Mom growled, or maybe groaned.

Peter rubbed his beard. "What do Christians in your world do for Bibles since that Group destroys them?"

Way waved. "Oh, that's no problem for The Group. The Group took the old manuscripts and re-translated them. The Group found the old ones to be judgmental and non-inclusive. The Group said the old ones could leave people feeling bad about themselves, so The Group fixed it."

Mom growled, or groaned, again. Way thought she would hit him.

Peter sidled up to Mom and put his arm around her. "Remember this boy's been brought up under complete control of this monster for his whole life. Don't be too hard on him."

"A mistake to bring him in," Abe called from the back of the cave. "A huge mistake."

Peter closed his eyes and let out a breath. "On that note, why don't we let you and that boy get some sleep." He moved toward four teenage girls that encircled and played with the baby. "Excuse me, ladies, but we need to get this boy and his daddy to bed. They've had quite the night."

Chapter 3—Mountain Jack

About three hours later, Way still hadn't fallen asleep. To his surprise, he missed the soothing droning of Grand Matron Filleen Tannon telling him how The Group would take care of his every need and how The Group knew what was best for him, among other things. Part of his problem in getting to sleep could have also been attributed to the fact that he was lying on a tattered blanket that covered a bed of dead leaves. It was the first night in his life that he had slept on anything other than a Group-issued mattress. He laid on his back, interlocked his fingers behind his head, and stared at the darkness of the cave ceiling. The baby slept beside him, taking easy breaths.

Way's mind wandered. Had he done the right thing in escaping the city with the baby? Would it be possible for him to go to The Group representatives in the city, turn the baby in, repent, and go on as if nothing had happened? No.

The baby stretched and smacked his lips. He smiled.

Way's mind returned to the questions. Had he done the right thing in escaping the city? For that moment, his answer to his own question was yes. He turned on his side and pulled the baby close. Yes. But he still missed Grand Matron Tannon's soothing voice.

Commotion started at the cave opening, which was covered by branches and leaves. Two watchmen were posted just outside.

"Who's there?" Way heard one of the watchmen say in a loud whisper.

Way couldn't make out the muffled response.

The watchmen along with a third person and a dog rushed through the branches and leaves, apparently not caring who they awakened. The watchmen each held to the third person, helping him as he stumbled along.

"Peter! Peter!" One of the watchmen, obviously knowledgeable of the sleeping arrangements in the cave, went to Peter's sleeping spot.

Peter had stirred at the first whispers and didn't seem to take long to be fully awake and aware. "What is it, Allen? What's wrong?"

"It's Mountain Jack," Allen said. "It's Mountain Jack, and there's trouble."

Way sat up. The cave was abuzz.

The one they called Mountain Jack tried to speak, but didn't have the breath.

Peter stood and helped Allen and the other watchman ease Mountain Jack into Peter's sleeping spot. Peter knelt beside Mountain Jack. "What is it, Jack? What's going on?"

Mountain Jack's shoulders heaved up and down, up and down. Not only was he out of breath, he sobbed. After a couple of minutes, he took one final big breath and let it out. "It was terrible, Pete. Terrible."

"What's that, Jack? What happened."

"Me and Shamus was out for our nightly hunt, and when we got back to the community, we seen several what I took to be government men at our camp. Me and Shamus stayed in the woods and watched." Mountain Jack pulled the dog close. "He did so good, Pete. My boy did good. He kept quieter than I did."

Peter patted Shamus. "That doesn't surprise me. He's a good one."

Jack sniffed and rubbed his sleeve across his nose. He sobbed. "Anyways, them government fellows, they lined up my community, had them get down on their knees and gunned them down. Most of them, anyways. Like they wasn't nothing but animals. Nothing but animals. Like I say, most of them they gunned down. Put the rifles to the back of they heads and pulled the triggers, like it weren't nothing. They didn't kill Arthur nor Mike nor Ozzy nor Yates, you know, our leaders. They said something about taking them back to the city and making examples out of them. Said they'd be good ones for one of them public extinguishings, they called it."

Several of the women cried. A couple of the men fell to their knees.

"Why?" Peter said. He gazed toward Way and the baby, who by that time was being held by one of the teenage girls. "Oh, no. God, please, no."

Jack sniffled again. "What is it? What you thinking?"

Peter got down on one knee. "What else did you hear those men say, Jack?"

Jack and Way locked eyes. Jack motioned toward him. "Who's the new fellow? Is he …? Those government fellows, they said something about hunting for a guy …," he paused, looking toward the girl holding the baby, "… and an offspring, they said."

Way shrunk back. All eyes were on him. He wished he could hide. "I …, I …," he stammered. No more words came. No more thoughts came.

"Is he the one they was looking for?" Jack asked.

Abe made his way from the back of the cave to join the others. He nodded repeatedly. "I knew it. I knew it. We should've left him out there. We had no business getting involved. Some of our best friends are dead, or as good as dead, because of him and that kid. We should have left them out there."

Several in the cave murmured.

Peter stroked his beard. "Quiet, please, everybody." He put a thumb and forefinger to his eyes and rubbed hard. "This is on me. It's not on him and the baby. I did what I thought was right."

Abe waved. "There's folks dead now because of him. We need to turn him loose. We can't have those world government men wandering around the woods." With fire in his eyes, he stepped toward Peter. "Do you want to end up like Art or Ozzy or them? Do you want to be taken to the city to be made an example? To have your head lopped off?"

"Abe." Jack was calm.

Abe continued his tirade.

"Abe," Jack said, still calm.

Abe finally stopped and looked open-mouthed at Jack.

"You can't cut them loose, Abe." Jack stood. "I would've done the same. Arthur would've done the same. Oz would've done the same. They all would've done the same." He grasped Abe's shoulder. "We can't ever stop helping. We can't ever stop caring. If they's someone out there, we got to do what we can to help."

Way's eyes moved to Abe. He appeared humbled. But from what he'd seen so far that night, Way didn't know how long that would last. Way finally found some words. He walked to the girl holding the baby and took him. "Maybe we should go. I didn't mean to endanger anyone. It's best if we make it on our own. If we get caught, we get caught."

"You'll do no such thing!" Mom stepped from among the crowd and not so gently took the baby. "It's certain death out there for you one way or the other, either them government goons getting you or freezing yourself to death when winter comes. You need to take care of this baby and yourself. He needs you."

Way moved to the cave opening, but stayed inside behind the dead limbs, leaves, and weeds that covered it. He moved aside some of the brush and peered into the darkness. "I don't want to put all of you at risk."

"We're at risk every day," Peter said. "Have been for years. Will be as long as we're on this earth."

"You've been out here for years?"

"Yep," Peter said. "As soon as we saw this whole Group thing coming, we hit the woods."

"All of you, together?"

"It wasn't this bunch. I left the city with my parents and some of their friends, some people we went to church with. By the grace of God, we met up with Mom and her husband; Allen and his parents; Tom and Denise, and others along the way. We started our little group and eventually met up with Jack and his group. They've been our neighbors for several years in one place and another."

"'One place and another'?"

Peter chuckled as he rubbed the back of his neck. "We've done a lot of moving over the years, always trying to stay as many steps ahead of the thugs as we can."

"Should you be telling him all this, Pete?" Abe joined the conversation. "How do you know he's not one of them? How do you know they didn't send him out here to help catch us?"

Way thought Abe's humbling would last longer. Apparently not.

Peter hung his head and palmed his face. He took a breath. "It's all right, Abe. You were with me when we found him and the baby in the woods. There's no way he was putting on an act."

Way's heart rate rose. The Group had spent countless hours trying to get him and other world citizens to keep their emotions in check. He'd let his emotions get the best of him when he ran away, and now Abe seemed to be doing everything he could to cause it to happen again. Way tightened his hands into fists, then relaxed them. Tightened. Relaxed. Tightened. Relaxed. "I promise you, Abe. I am in no way trying to lead the Corpsmen to you. I don't want them to find you. I don't even know you people. I have no reason to do you harm."

Abe scoffed. His head bobbed. "What else are you going to say?"

Way didn't know what time it was when Peter woke him the next morning. "Is it six o'clock already?"

Peter shrugged. "No clocks, man, but I'm sure it's well past six. I haven't been out, but I'd guess seven or eight."

"Seven or eight?" Way ruffled his hair. "I haven't slept that late since I was a child."

"What?"

"At home, the alarm for day workers goes off at six. We have to be at our purpose by seven." Way paused. "That reminds me, who brings us food?"

"Brings us food?"

"It's time for breakfast. Back home, food service brings breakfast by six-fifteen."

"Good luck with that." Peter motioned taking in the cave from one end to the other. "You see all the people in here? They're food service. We're all food service. We each play a part in providing the meals. Some of us plant and harvest. Some hunt or trap. Some catch. Some cook. We all pitch in."

Way curled his lip and flared a nostril. "Hunt, trap, or catch? What do you eat?"

"Whatever we can come up with." Peter chuckled. "Catch as catch can, man. We have squirrel, rabbit, deer, fish, a fair amount of fruits and vegetables. Whatever we come up with."

Way wrinkled his nose. "Squirrel, rabbit, fish, and deer? That's meat."

Peter smiled. "There's some debate on whether fish is meat." He put his fingers to his chest. "I think it is, but there are a lot of people a lot smarter than me that say it isn't. Or at least they said that back when people could communicate and read and so on."

Way blinked. "I've never eaten meat. The Group doesn't allow it. The Group says, first, we should never kill another living, breathing creature for our gain. Second, The Group says meat's not good for us."

Peter kicked at the cave floor, "Your Group's never had a good steak. That's what I'd say." With that, he motioned Mountain Jack to join him and Way. "That Group doesn't allow people to eat meat, Jack. What do you think of that?"

Jack sneered and blustered. His thick brown-gray beard danced up and down as he spoke. "I'd say that's the biggest bunch of foolishness I ever heard. A man that don't eat meat ain't much more than a rabbit."

Peter kept his arm draped over Jack's shoulders. "Good answer. That's what I like to hear. Now, for the real reason I called you over. And this is a hard one."

Jack pursed his lips and dipped his head. "Uh-huh."

"I know this is hard for you, but would you mind us going to your camp to see if there's anything we can use?"

"That'd be fine," Jack said. "In fact, I believe that's what they'd want. That stuff ain't going to do them no good no more. Someone ought to get some use out of it."

"Thanks." Peter pulled Jack closer. "I appreciate that. We all appreciate that." He released Jack and stood square in front of him. "Some of us will go over there tonight after dark and see what we can find."

Abe ambled over. "You sure that's a good idea?" He gestured. "Those government men might still be snooping around on the lookout for this fellow and the baby. Wouldn't it be better to wait until they've quit searching?"

Peter gestured as he spoke. "You might have something there. But also, with their satellites and all, they can pretty much see us any time we're out. If they wanted, they could send their goons and get us. All that stuff was well advanced when we left the city. I can only imagine how far along it is now."

"He's right, you know." Way had listened, but finally added to the conversation. He glanced toward the four teenage girls sitting in a circle, joking and laughing, several feet away. If he hadn't known better from what he'd seen so far in the cave, he wouldn't have known they had any worries. He turned his attention back to the men with him. "That's how they find rebels like you. Sometimes they go after them hard for several months, and sometimes they leave them alone for years. They've increased their efforts recently. The Group thinks it's getting down to the last few rebels, and people are hungry for all of them, well, all of you, to be taken in."

"I believe they got that one-world government so many people wanted for so long," Peter said.

Way scratched his nose. "I don't know what you're talking about, but I do know The Group takes care of everyone, provides us with everything we need."

Peter motioned toward a book lying on Mom's pallet. "The Bible there told us something like this was coming."

Way narrowed his eyes and wrinkled his nose. "Seriously? If people come to that conclusion from reading that book, no wonder The Group burns them and performs a cleansing on anyone found with an old one in their possession."

Mom moved from the back of the cave and had her finger in Way's face faster than he would have imagined she could. "Boy, I was all for taking you and your baby in. I'm all for us helping you in every we can, but do not ever let me hear you disparaging God's word again."

Way shrunk back. He had an inkling about how Abe felt the night before. "I, uh, yes, ma'am, whatever you say." He lowered his eyes.

Arms crossed and wrinkled lips pursed, Mom looked Way over from head to toe. She grunted. "Uh-huh. Look, son, we love you and your boy. You two are part of our group." She made a circular motion. The sagging skin on her chin flapped as she spoke. "Our group, not that Group you keep talking about. We're going to take care of you and that boy, whether you all like it or not."

Way blinked. "You don't even know us."

Mom jabbed a thumb toward the Bible. "That book tells me I'm supposed to love you, your baby, even the people in that Group."

Way rocked back and forth. "Love's not something we hear a lot about in the city."

"That's cause they ain't got God in your city," Mom said. "He got booted out."

"Amen." Mountain Jack hooked his thumbs around the straps of his too-small overalls. "She tells the truth, boy." He caught himself. "Say, I don't reckon we been properly introduced. I didn't catch your name." He held out a meaty hand and stubby fingers. "I'm Jack. Guess you caught that they call me Mountain Jack."

With reluctance, Way responded by reaching out to Jack. "I'm Way March."

"Well, a pox on all of us," Peter said with a smile. "We made it through the whole night without any introductions. It took the roughest one of us all to bring some civilization to this whole meeting."

"I'm the most refined one around here." Jack threw back his shoulders and puffed out his chest. "If it weren't for me, you 'uns wouldn't have no culture at all." He turned to Way. "How about your boy, there. What's his name?"

Way narrowed his eyes. He studied the baby who at that time was the center of attention for many of the women of the community. "Actually, he doesn't have one. Today is his first birthday. Today he was either going to get his name from The Group or get extinguished. I ran because I didn't want him to get extinguished, but that's what my domestic partner, Luka, planned to do. She thought he was too much trouble and would hinder her work for The Group."

Mom stroked her chin and studied the baby. "So he doesn't have a name? And he was supposed to get one today?" Mom smiled and clapped. "What say we give him one?"

Others voiced their approval of Mom's idea.

Way hesitated. "Um. I don't know if we should. The Group takes care of that."

"Come on." Jack tugged at the weathered John Deere cap that Way figured he wore every waking hour. "Your Group ain't here. You ought to man up and name the boy."

Way's eyes darted about the cave. "But The Group takes care of that. Giving him an unauthorized name could be big trouble."

"You ran away from the city and all that control. I don't imagine you could be in much more trouble," Jack said. "Your life ain't worth nothing as it is. Not naming the boy ain't going to help your cause none. I say give the boy a name."

Even the teenage girls had turned their attention to the conversation and seemed to favor naming the baby.

Peter looked around the cave. "Way, I'd say everyone is pretty much in agreement that you need to name the boy. What'll it be? What are you going to do?"

"The Group takes care of that."

Peter pressed his palms together with his fingers pointing up. "I understand your concern, but like it or not, you're not part of whatever goes on in the city, or whatever that Group does. You made your decision when you ran away with the baby. It doesn't matter if you believe like we do or not. It doesn't matter if you still want that Group to take care of you or not. You're in this thing with both feet and up to your eyeballs. You might as well name the baby."

"Here, here," Jack said. "And, by the way, you might as well name him Jack. That's capital J, small a-c-k."

Peter gave Jack a playful shove to the shoulder.

"What you going to name him?" Mom asked as she touched Way's back.

"I, I don't have any idea. The Group takes care of that."

"Stop worrying about your precious Group and name the kid," Abe said. "My goodness. You're your own man now. Think for yourself."

"I don't even know where to start."

Mom retrieved the Bible from her pallet. "There's a whole gaggle of good names in here." On the way back to join Way and the others, Mom stopped in her tracks. "I got the perfect name. How about Moses?"

Way flared a nostril. "What kind of name is that?"

"My goodness!" Abe turned and went toward the back of the cave.

Mom watched Abe. "Tsk. Tsk. That boy." She smiled at Way. "I guess you wouldn't know. Let me tell you what kind of name it is."

Mom started with the children of Israel being enslaved by Egypt. She went into how Pharaoh ordered all Jewish male children killed and told how Moses's mother put him in a basket and released it into the Nile River. She finished with Moses leading the children of Israel out of captivity.

"So I think with you escaping to save his life, that fits the story of Moses," Mom concluded.

Way considered Mom's story. "Hmm." He raised and lowered one shoulder. "I guess that sounds as good as anything." He went to the baby and picked him up. "Come here, Moses." Smiling, he held Moses close. "What do you think of that? You got a name today after all."

Moses cooed. He grabbed Way's nose.

Way twisted from side to side. He held Moses tighter. "So, how's it feel? You're no longer 'the offspring.' You're Moses." Way stopped. He wiped his eye and sniffled.

A tear ran down Mom's face. "I'm just an old softie. If I knew you good enough I'd give you a hug."

"We don't do a lot of hugging in the city. Not that The Group forbids it. I don't know. We just don't do a lot of it."

Mom caressed Moses's face. "That's all right." She took him from Way and hugged him. "We'll teach this boy to be a hugger."

"That's fine," Way said. "I don't mind him being a hugger. The Group taught us to be open-minded. We're receptive to most anything."

"Except Christians!" Abe called from the back of the cave.

Mom waved off Abe's remark. "Let's not worry about him right now. This is a happy day. We're not going to let him dampen our spirits."

Shamus, Jack's dog, nuzzled up to Jack. Jack rubbed the dog's head.

"Can I ask something?" Way said.

"Sure," Peter said. "Ask away."

"Why do you have that creature with you?" Way asked Jack.

Jack scratched Shamus behind the ear. "He's my buddy, my companion. Me and him been together a long time. We been through a lot together."

"Does he belong to you?"

Jack's face lit up and his eyes sparkled as he patted Shamus. "I don't know if that fully captures how much this ol' boy means to me, but I guess you could say that."

"The Group would not like that," Way said.

"What you talking about?" Jack continued to pat Shamus.

"The Group says one creature should never belong to another. Every creature has the right to be free."

Peter sputtered. "'Every creature has the right to be free'?"

"Yes."

"You mean the way you're free?"

"Of course, I'm free. All world citizens are free. The Group takes care of us and sees that we eat and have clothes and shelter. So yes, The Group takes care of all our needs, but we are free."

"How stupid can you be?" Abe was still at the back of the cave.

"What's that?"

"You ain't free," Abe said. "I don't know where you got that cockamamie idea, but someone played you for a fool if you think you're free."

Way looked around. "You think you're free? You live in a cave, hiding from Corpsmen just waiting for the day they come and get you. You don't know when you'll eat again or what you'll eat."

Abe stormed from the back of the cave. He looked ready to fight.

Peter stepped in front of Abe and prevented him from reaching Way. He pressed each of their chests. "Hold on, fellows. We can't worry about who's free and who's not. We're all in this together. We have a community to take care of. We can't let that Group or its thugs or anyone or anything else keep us from what we have to do. Now, I'd suggest you two go your separate ways until it's time to scavenge Jack's old campsite, then you'll both go with Jack and me. One way or another, you two are going to get along."

Abe pressed his lips together tightly and flared his nostrils. He turned and marched to the back of the cave.

Glad and relieved that Abe hadn't punched him, Way tried to calm himself. He'd never been in a physical altercation. The Group would never approve of such activity. He laid on his pallet and turned his back to Peter and Jack. "Let me know when you're ready to go."

Chapter 4—Scavenging

That night, Way, Peter, Jack, Allen, Abe, and Shamus prepared to go scavenging at Jack's community.

With Shamus by his side, Jack ambled to Way's pallet. "Say, there, bud, did you happen to get out of there with a gun?"

Way was taken aback. "A gun? What are you talking about?"

Jack held up his thumb and pointed his forefinger. "You know, a gun. Pow. Pow. Did you get out of there with one?"

Leaning back, Way tucked his chin. "Oh, I didn't have access to a weapon. No one does. The Group would never go for that. The only ones who get weapons are the Corpsmen. And that is only when they're on duty."

"That figures."

"Do you have a weapon?"

"If you mean guns or rifles, no," Jack said. "Most people I've known out here left the city with guns, but we haven't had any ammo for years. We're basically down to knives, clubs, bows and arrows and whatever else we can come up with."

An hour or so later, Jack led the way through the woods to his old community. He stopped behind a tree and motioned for the others to do the same. He leaned around the tree and peered through the darkness into the community.

Way had never seen anything like it. Unlike the community that found him the previous night which stayed in a cave divided into several rooms, this community had a series of structures. Rough structures. Very rough structures. In the city, all he had ever seen was the gray pods where people lived and the gray buildings where they worked. "What is all that?" He asked no one particular.

"Shh." Jack held up a finger. Once he had the quiet he wanted, he pointed toward a cluster of the structures. "Those are lean-tos. As you see, they're open on three sides." He pointed to other structures. "Those are huts. A little more developed than the lean-tos. Maybe like what we used to call more high-tech."

"People live in those things?"

"Yep," Jack said.

"How can they live in those conditions?"

"Well, like my daddy used to say, 'You do what you got to do.' He was a wise man." Jack smiled, but then went serious. He looked from Way to Peter to Abe to Allen. "We have to make this quick. Those thugs may be wandering around out here. They were not at all happy about our friend here escaping."

Way looked warily about. The noises of the night were foreign to him. He knew of no night noises in the city. Once he was in the pod by 7 p.m., he was there until 6:45 the next morning when he left for his task at the Preservation Center. If there were night noises in the city, the only ones who heard them were night workers. And, he never talked to, or even saw, night workers. "What's all that noise?"

"Well, son," Jack said, "that's frogs croaking and crickets chirping. I heard a hoot owl a bit ago. You can hear all sorts of things out here."

"What's a frog or, what did you say, a cricket?"

Abe huffed. "My goodness."

Allen knelt and squinted, looking toward the community's structures. "Give him some grace, Abe. He's been in that city his whole life, just learning what they want him to learn. If you were to take a trip into that place, there'd probably be plenty of things that left you wondering. We're all ignorant, just on different subjects."

"Hmph." Abe made his feelings clear.

"That's enough, Abe," Peter said. "Now, Jack, is there any of these places you think would be better than the others for gathering?"

Jack stroked his beard. "Well, Pete, I reckon, one's 'bout as good as another. There'll be some that have one thing and some that have another."

"Okay, then." Peter cracked his knuckles. "Let's split up. Way and Allen, you come with me. Jack, you, Abe, and Shamus go together. We have to make it quick. Those guards could come around any time."

"Sounds good." Jack tapped Abe on the shoulder. "Let's go." He pointed toward a hut. "We'll check out Arthur's hut and see what him and his family might've had that can help us."

Way watched Jack, Abe, and Shamus leave for the hut.

Peter started the other direction. "We'll go over here and see what we find."

They went to a lean-to. Peter and Allen rummaged through the goods. Way stood to the side, watching.

Peter raised a flannel shirt. "Surely, this'll fit someone back home."

Allen dug under a couple of blankets. He pulled out a knife and took it from its sheath. "Yes." He held it up to examine it in the moonlight. "We can never have too many of these babies."

"You're going to take that?" Way asked.

"Course, I am, man." Allen smiled. "On second thought, here." He tossed the knife to Way.

Way bumbled with it a couple of seconds, and it fell to the ground.

Allen chuckled. "Not much of a ballplayer, are you?"

"What are you talking about?"

Allen lifted the blankets and shook them. "We should probably take these." He looked at Way. "You know, baseball? Football? Basketball?"

With one foot, Way scooted the knife away. "I don't know what you're talking about."

Allen stopped in mid-shake. "Sports? Athletics? Competition?"

"Whatever those things are," Way said, "we don't do them."

"Don't do sports? That's un-American."

"Uh, Allen," Peter rummaged through a backpack, "I think pretty much everything about the new world is un-American. That's kind of why we live in the woods."

Allen snorted. "I guess that's right." He turned his attention back to Way. "How come you don't do sports?"

Way took a step back from the knife. "I wouldn't know. The Group probably just doesn't think they are beneficial to personkind."

Peter stopped rummaging and turned slowly toward Way. "How could they think sports aren't beneficial?"

"What do you do in these sports?" Way asked.

Peter scratched his head. "You get two people or teams, two groups of people, and you go against each other, see who can get the most points, runs, goals, whatever. Whoever has the highest score wins. At least in most cases, the idea is to get the highest score. Some games, like golf, you want the lowest score."

"Ah," Way said. "I kind of get the idea, and I see why The Group may not have us do these things. It could be if one team or individual has a higher, what you call, score than another team or individual, the one that has the low score may feel bad about themselves or himself or herself. The Group wants everyone to feel good and be equal. No one is better than anyone else. We are all the same."

Allen grunted. "Never heard the like. Back in my day, people thought competition was a good thing. It taught you how to deal with winning and losing, how to be a good sport, how to deal with adversity, how to overcome obstacles."

Way waved. "Oh, we don't have to worry about adversity or obstacles. The Group took care of that. The Group takes care of everything. All we have to do is make our contributions as world citizens."

"I'm afraid this Group has you snookered," Allen said as he rifled through a pile of clothes.

"Snookered?"

"Yeah, you know, hoodwinked, blinded."

"How so?"

"They have you thinking they're good for you, but actually they're about the worst thing that ever happened." Allen held up a pair of blue jeans. He tossed them to Way. "These may fit you."

Unlike the knife, Way managed to catch the jeans. He held them up and inspected them in the moonlight. "Why would I want these? They have holes in the knees."

Peter held up one pant leg. "You would want them because it could come to the point of having these or having nothing. We don't have your Group dropping off clothes for us. We have to be happy with whatever we can scavenge. That may be the best pair of pants you see for two years."

Allen scoffed. "Or more."

Peter nodded. "Yep. Or more."

"I guess I'll take them." Way folded the jeans.

Mountain Jack and Abe, with Shamus, hurried to the lean-to. Jack went to one knee beside Shamus and turned to look back into the darkness.

"What is it, Jack?" Peter asked.

Jack stroked Shamus's back and continued scouring the area from which he and Abe had come. "We got to get out of here, Pete. We heard someone."

Abe caught his breath. "Several someones even. I wager it's some of them government thugs."

Peter muttered.

Allen picked up the knife he had tried to give Way. He slid it in his pants pocket. He eyed Way. "I hope you can move through the woods."

Way's heart pattered. "I don't know. I guess I can try."

"Let's go," Peter said in a throaty whisper. He led the men and Shamus into the woods.

"Who's there?" a man called from behind.

"I think they're this way," said a second man.

Shamus stopped and turned around toward the voices. He growled and the hair on his back stood.

"Keep him quiet!" Abe whispered. "He's going to get us killed."

Jack patted Shamus on the head. "Quiet, boy. I'm sure they got us outnumbered and outgunned."

Peter motioned ahead. "Come on. We have to keep moving, and we need to go the opposite direction of home. We can't take a chance on leading them there."

Behind them, lights flashed through the night. There were more than Way could count in a quick glimpse. He stepped over a fallen tree, and his foot caught in a vine. He stumbled to all fours.

Abe grabbed Way by the shirt and yanked him to his feet. "Hurry! You're making more noise than that old dog. Between the two of you, we don't have a chance."

"This way," a man said from behind. Way noticed the voice was not one of the ones he heard earlier.

Peter stopped. He grabbed Jack and pulled him forward. "You take the lead, Jack. You know this area better than I do."

"You got it, brother." Jack ducked under a branch and went to the left. "There's a lake over here. If we can get there maybe we can make it."

"I don't know why I ever left my pod," Way said. "If I'd stayed there, none of this would be happening. I wish I was back in my pod."

"And your boy would be dead," Peter said. "No need to worry about any of that now. What's done is done, and you're in this too deep to turn back."

Way wiped sweat from his forehead and stepped over a small bush. "Maybe I should just go to them and turn myself in. Maybe they would let the rest of you go."

Peter kept close behind Jack. "Not a chance. They're like sharks after blood now. Your life won't be worth two cents if they get you. On top of that, your boy needs a daddy. Even if you don't want out of this for your sake, you need to get out of it for his."

Way heard muffled voices from behind. They seemed farther away than they had been a couple of minutes earlier.

"You know, he may have something there, Peter," Abe said. "If he turns himself in maybe it would at least buy us some time."

Peter stopped in his tracks and wheeled around to face Abe. He stuck a finger a couple of inches from Abe's nose. "Not an option."

"We're almost there." Jack knelt beside a fallen oak tree.

Peter, Abe, Allen, and Way knelt beside him.

"I heard someone!" called a voice from behind.

Way was sure it was closer.

"This way!"

Way knew it was closer. He heard several people moving through the woods.

"I think they're over here."

They were closer.

Way heard his heart beating.

The pursuers shined flashlights through the darkness. "How much longer are we going to look?"

"Let's give it a little longer. They have to be around here somewhere."

Way moved closer to the log. He leaned a cheek against it. Corpsmen were in his line of sight, only about twenty feet away and getting closer.

Seconds later, the Corpsmen were just a few feet on the other side of the log.

"Let's give up for now and go back to base."

"What do we tell the captain?"

"We can make something up. They'll send us out again tomorrow anyway."

"All right. If you say so. You can make it up. You're the one in charge of this expedition."

"No problem. I'm creative. My second purpose possibility was working in the Information Center and writing news for the masses. It just so happened that my career test score dictated that I become a Corpsman. So what was I to do? Oh, well. Let's get everyone gathered and go back."

The two men started calling to their peers and got them together. When the Corpsmen reunited, they compared notes and finally left the area.

Way and the others kept quiet. It took several minutes for the knots in Way's stomach to disappear.

Jack stood and leaned heavily on the log. "That was a close one, boys."

"We still need to be careful," Peter said. "That might have been a ruse to draw us out."

Way's legs shook. He could hardly stand.

Peter tugged at his beard. "Well, let's get home. I don't think I want to chance scavenging anymore tonight."

"Yeah, I'm afraid I'm all scavenged out." Jack rubbed Shamus's neck.

An hour later, the five men and Shamus trudged through the woods back to the cave.

As they neared the cave, Way smelled smoke. Fire had devoured the brush that covered the cave opening.

"No!" Abe took two quick steps toward the cave.

Allen grabbed Abe by the shirt. "Wait, Abe! You don't know who might be there. I'm worried about my family, too, but we have to wait."

Seeing Abe stopped kept Way from running to the cave to check on Moses.

"But Mom was in there." Abe clutched his hair. "I have to see if she's all right. I have to get Mom."

Peter took Abe in a hug. "I know it's tough, but we have to wait. Like I said in the woods, we have to be careful. There could be government men all over the place."

Abe went to his knees. Then down to all fours.

Chapter 5—Message From Filleen

The men waited about half an hour.

Abe sat with his legs crossed, elbows resting on his knees, and his chin laying heavy on his folded hands. "You think we can go look? I got to find out about Mom."

Peter rocked from one foot to the other. "Maybe. I haven't seen or heard anything to make me think government men are around. What do you think, Jack? You know more about that sort of thing than I do."

Jack rubbed the back of his neck. "I don't know, Pete. I guess we can give it a try. I haven't picked up on anything to make me think them thugs are around. I reckon if they come in on us, we can go down fighting. Won't take long to go down, but we can fight."

Summoning something he never knew he had, Way took a deep breath. "Let's go. I need to check on the offspring, uh, Moses."

Peter reached out to help Abe to his feet. "We all had people we care about in there. I guess now's as good a time as any to see what happened."

Once the men and Shamus were in the cave, there was no Mom, no Moses, and no anyone else. Cave walls were blackened by smoke.

The men looked frantically through the cave. Signs of struggle were evident throughout, a pot that had contained stew was overturned, blankets and clothes appeared to have been thrown, a knife with dried blood lay near Peter's bedding.

Jack sat on his haunches and drew meaningless squiggles in the dirt. Shamus sat beside Jack and pressed his nose into his side.

Peter lay on his bedding.

Abe sat on the dirt floor. He held Mom's blanket close.

Allen wandered about the cave. He went into the area that had been petitioned off for his family.

Way sat on the pallet that had been made for him his first night. He noticed something just inside of and off to the side of the cave opening. He went and picked it up. It was a black, metal box still warm from the fire, but undamaged.

Way undid the clasp and opened the box. He pulled out a small device.

"What you got there?" Jack asked.

Way examined the device. "It's a video player."

The other men gathered around.

Jack scratched his head. "What do you do with it?"

Even with all the trials they faced, Allen chuckled. "I'd say you play videos on it. You do remember videos and such, don't you?"

"I never did go in much for that type of thing," Jack said.

Abe raised his eyebrows. "I was born out here. I don't know the first thing about what you all are talking about."

Peter pointed at the device. "You know how to operate that thing, Way?"

"Yeah. I've used them a few times over the years. Mostly The Group communicates through televisions, computers, and other messaging systems, but sometimes we have to use these."

"Why is it here?" Peter said.

Way flipped open the player and studied it. "With everything that's happened, I'd say The Group has something to tell us."

Jack stepped closer. "What is it? What is it?"

"Hmm." Way fiddled with some buttons. "Give me just a minute and we should see." He turned on the player and pushed a couple of buttons.

The machine's tiny screen flickered to life. The Group logo appeared.

Way held the player. The other men stepped closer and stood shoulder to shoulder.

Way pressed another button, and after a couple of seconds a woman appeared on screen. "It's Grand Matron Tannon."

Filleen Tannon wore a blue dress and a string of pearls. She sat at a mahogany desk. "Good day, gentlemen. By now, I'm sure you have figured out that we have your friends and families. As I speak, they are resting comfortably in their cells. Tomorrow they will be given the opportunity to renounce the man, Jesus, in the form they believe in him and embrace the way of The Group.

"If they do not choose the way of The Group, they will face horrors beyond anything you gentlemen who have been in the woods all these years can imagine. Maybe Mr. March will be good enough to share with you what your loved ones will face." She offered a tight-lipped smile.

Abe motioned toward the player. "What's she talking about?"

"Yeah, man, what's that all about?" Allen asked.

"What does she mean about horrors?" Jack asked.

Way paused the video and lowered the player. "Well, when The Group captures people like you, it gives them the chance to switch. Some do and some don't."

Peter closed his eyes and took in a breath. "You mean they get some people to turn from Jesus?"

"Yes. Most don't, but there are some that do. But it's not like they have to totally quit believing in him. They can still be Christians. They just have to give up the notion that he's the only way to get to Heaven."

"But he is," Peter said.

Palms up, Way shrugged. "That's what you say. There are those who think different."

Peter rocked back and forth. "Probably best that we don't get into this right now. Tell us what will happen to our people."

"When The Group captures people like you, it gives them the chance to turn away from your beliefs. The Group makes a big deal out of it. Everyone is either to attend the ceremony or watch on television or computer. The Group wants to make sure every world citizen sees it."

Jack tugged at the bill of his cap. "You mean you've been to or seen these here so-called ceremonies?"

"Oh, yeah." Way nodded. "All world citizens have. Well, all those who didn't turn their backs on the World Community."

"Say what?" Abe made a fist.

"I'm just telling you how it is," Way said.

Allen patted Abe on the back. "Calm down, man. Just let him tell us about this deal."

Abe's jaw muscles tightened and relaxed. He narrowed his eyes. "Go ahead."

Way relaxed. "Let me put it another way. How about all world citizens have seen them except those who didn't agree with The Group's way of doing things?"

Abe grunted. "I guess that'll do."

Peter made a circular motion. "Go on, Way."

"Like I said, The Group makes a big deal out of it. The crowd gathers and gets worked into a frenzy. The Group brings the rebels out one by one and offers them the chance to come to our side."

"And if they don't?" Peter leaned close to Way.

"They put them through a lot. It's for the rebels' own good, though. The Group wants to bring them in to its way. The Group would much rather convert them than hurt them."

"What do the spectators do when this is going on?" Allen asked. "What did you do when you watched this?"

"The crowd would go wild. The more the rebels resisted, the more the crowd yelled. They thrilled at seeing the torture increa—," he had started to enjoy recounting the events, but stopped and thought where he was and who he was with.

Peter pointed at Way. "And what did you do?"

Way looked to the ground. He shifted his weight. "I, I'm afraid I enjoyed it. I don't know. I got caught up in the excitement."

Peter tilted his head to one side. "You do know those were people you were watching being tortured? Actual flesh and blood human beings, not animals."

"Oh, The Group would never treat animals the way it treats rebels."

"Do you hear what you're saying?" Peter said. "Don't you see a problem with that thinking?"

"They're just rebels," Way said. He thought for a few seconds. "That's the way The Group puts it anyway. We respect animals. They deserve to be treated with respect."

Abe took a step toward Way, both fists clenched.

Allen stepped between them and pressed on Abe's chest. "Calm down. Calm down. He doesn't know any better."

Abe pushed Allen away and took a step back. "Maybe a good, sharp slap upside the head will help him know better."

Peter pressed his palms toward the cave floor. "Allen's right. We need to calm down." He jabbed a thumb toward Way. "He's had a lifetime of indoctrination by this Group. He's been with us about thirty hours. Even if, by the grace of God, we're able to get him free of everything they've put in his head, it's going to take some time."

Abe grunted. "Well, I hope God speeds it up. If he don't, I may have to punch this boy in the face."

"There ain't going to be no punching anyone in the face." Jack took hold of Abe's thick upper arm. "Look, son. We have a tough life out here, and the screws have been turned tighter in the last day or so, but we got to keep Jesus up front."

Abe pulled away from Jack's grasp. He wiped a tear from his eye. "It's just hard, Jack. They got all your people. They got all our people. Now this joker tells us he enjoyed seeing our brothers and sisters tortured and that them and us are lower than animals."

Allen motioned for the others to step close to Way. "Maybe we should go on with the video."

"That's probably a good idea." Way started the player.

"There is no getting away," Filleen said. "We know where you are right now. If you leave your cave, we'll be able to track your movements. You are the last rebels. If you turn yourselves in and are willing to start thinking correctly, you can become productive world citizens." She interlocked her fingers. "Even if we capture you, I will be generous enough to give you a chance to join us. I'm more than happy to give the world five more mouths to feed. I believe The Group can manage that." She pointed at the screen. "And just to be sure you know, we can get you anytime we want."

She interlocked her fingers and held them at her chin. "Another thing, Mr. March, the offspring you ran away with has been extinguished. The Corpsmen took care of that little task before bringing all the others in. The offspring's mother had already informed us of her intention to take him to the Extinguishing Center. So, the Corpsmen, under my orders, extinguished him while in the woods. Your little episode was in vain, went for naught. You did nothing but prolong the inevitable and cost several of your new friends their lives in the process.

"On a final note, the one your little community so quaintly calls 'Mom' put up a good fight for her age. As you watch this, she is waiting in her cell. Tomorrow we will give her a chance to come to her senses. From what I hear from the those who were in on the search and capture, there's not much chance of that happening. As they said in days of old, she has a lot of spunk." Filleen chuckled. "Of course, spunk will only take you so far when you face the deliverer." She nodded. "And rest assured, gentlemen, all of you will face him before long."

The screen went black.

Abe looked to Peter. "Now what?"

Peter stroked his beard. "We need to get out of here."

"Moses has been extinguished?" Way dropped the video player. "How could they do that? I didn't want that."

"Well, get it in your head good, bud." Mountain Jack grabbed the bill of his cap. "That's the kind of people you're dealing with in that Group bunch. If someone is an inconvenience, they kill them. If someone crosses them, they kill them. If someone don't see things their way, they kill them."

"I don't know. I just don't know." Way sighed. "How could they do that? He never hurt anyone."

Peter tilted his head. "Kind of like Jack said, he inconvenienced your wife, she told that Group he inconvenienced her, and they killed him. Don't you see? In general, they don't care about individuals. You're just a cog in the wheel to them."

Abe shifted from side to side and jabbed a thumb toward the cave opening. "Could we talk about this on the move? The lady said they know where we are. They could show up any minute."

"What are we going to do when they show up?" Allen looked from Peter to Jack and back.

"We fight." Peter tensed, then relaxed, his jaw. "I'd rather them kill me out here than let them get me in the city and make a spectacle out of me."

"Jack?" Allen asked.

"I'm with Pete." Jack gestured. "I say if they come after us, we take as many of them with us as we can."

Allen blinked. "What? How can you say that? We can't be judge, jury, and executioner. You kill one of them and you're sending them straight to Hell. That's not our job."

"Excuse me," Jack hooked a thumb around his overall strap, "but they're so far gone, they're going to Hell whether we send them there or not. And you know, we're not the ones sending them. They make their own choices."

Allen stalked away a few steps. He turned to face the others. "What if we witness to them? What if we could save even one?"

Peter exhaled. "Allen, brother, I'd say they made their choice long ago."

"That's just it." Allen fell back, leaning against the cave wall. "They haven't heard of Jesus. At least not the way we know him. They haven't heard the truth." He tilted his head toward Way. "They're brainwashed by this Group he's been talking about. They've never had a chance."

"The Bible has plenty of stories where God called his people to fight the enemy and destroy them." The vein running down the middle of Peter's forehead stood out.

Way looked to the ground and drew a line in the dirt with his toe. "There wasn't a lot of arguing in the city."

"That's Old Testament." Allen tugged at the unbuttoned flannel shirt he wore as an overshirt. "After Jesus came, it was God's love."

Peter scoffed. "Tell that to the folks in the Book of Revelation."

Allen became more animated. "How about 'turn the other cheek'? Who said that? Oh, yeah, Jesus."

"Fellows, fellows." Jack chuckled. "You could chase that squirrel around the tree all day and not catch it. I say just agree to disagree and move on."

Allen still leaned against the cave wall. "We can move on, but I'm not killing anybody."

Peter took a step back. "Have it your way, but what are you going do if it's them or you? Them or me?" He nodded toward Way. "What are you going to do if it's them or him?"

"As far as them or me, I hope I'll just let them take me peacefully. If it's them or one of you, well, I'll deal with that when the time comes," Allen said.

"Think about it hard, brother," Peter said. "That's a big question."

About half an hour later and still in the cave, the men had gathered all the supplies they could carry and were ready to leave.

Jack hummed as he fashioned an old shirt into a bag to carry a few items. He looked up with a start and put a finger to his mouth. "Shh. Listen. I hear something."

The others froze in their tracks.

Way heard rustling.

Peter gripped Allen's shoulder and whispered. "Brother, it might be about time for that big decision."

Jack unsheathed his knife. Abe grabbed an aluminum baseball bat. Peter held tight to a dead limb. He went to one side of the opening and stood with his back to the wall, neck craned. Allen stood in the middle of the cave.

Way was lost. Abe retrieved another aluminum baseball bat, gave it to Way, and went to stand beside Peter. Way studied the bat. He looked to the opening. There was more rustling. He was still lost.

"Boys?" came a voice from outside. "Abraham are you in there?"

"Mom?" Abe grabbed Peter. "It's Mom!"

Peter covered Abe's mouth. "Shh."

"Brother Peter?" the voice said. "Are you boys in there?"

Peter took a deep breath.

Way figured Peter might as well answer because whoever it was would probably come in anyway.

Apparently Peter agreed. "Yes, we're here."

"We're coming in." Mom stepped to the opening, holding Moses.

Moses squealed and reached for Way. There were hugs all around.

Way held Moses close. "Oh, it's so good to see you! I thought you were extinguished." Way's jaw went slack. He looked to Peter. "The Grand Matron told us he was extinguished and she was in a cell."

Jack sheathed his knife and stood as straight as his age and years of rugged life would allow. "Yes, she did, boy. She lied to you. She lied to all of us."

"What?" Way crinkled his forehead. "Lied? What's that?"

"Say what? You don't know what a lie is?" Peter said.

"My goodness!" Abe slapped his thighs. "He don't even know what a lie is. This guy is hopeless."

"Hold on, Abe." Peter stepped to Way. "Okay, what happened here is that grand matron lady told you something happened that didn't really happen. That's a lie."

"She told me something happened that didn't really happen, and that's a lie?"

"Yeah, bud," Jack joined in. "She told you something happened that didn't really happen. Haven't you ever done anything like that?"

Way hesitated. "Well, yes," he ran the back of his fingers down Moses's chubby cheek, "but that was always just to keep myself out of trouble with my domestic partner or the leader at my task. That's just something everyone does. There's nothing wrong with that. It doesn't hurt anyone."

"Well, your grand matron lied to you," Peter said, "and you see that it hurt you. It caused you sadness to think your boy was dead. It could have caused you to do something you wouldn't have done otherwise."

"That's right," Allen continued Peter's thought. "It could have caused you to turn yourself in to those Corpsmen, thinking they already had your boy, so you didn't have anything else to live for."

"Well …, but …," Way stammered. "Grand Matron Tannon wants the best for me. The Group wants the best for me."

Peter pursed his lips. "It's high time you consider the possibility that your grand matron and that Group bunch don't always shoot straight with you."

"'Shoot straight'?"

Jack spoke to Peter, but poked a thumb toward Way. "Remember, Pete, you're dealing with someone who doesn't know a thing about guns or weapons or such."

Peter chuckled and nodded. "True." He shifted his weight from one foot to the other and back again. "Okay. Here's the deal." He gestured as he spoke, apparently trying to help make his point. "If this Group has lied to you in this case to try to bring you harm, don't you think it's highly possible, likely even, that they've lied to you in the past?"

"In fact, bud," Jack toyed with the bill of his cap, "I'd wager that Group was and still is, telling people that things that did happen, didn't happen and vice versa."

Still holding Moses, Way took a step back. His shoulders slumped. He blinked. "But The Group takes care of us. It wants us to be free from the old, archaic ways. Wants us to be free from the wrongheaded thinking that was so prevalent in the past. Why would the grand matron tell me my son was extinguished?"

Peter drew a breath and raised his eyebrows. "Like Allen said, it could have been to get you to turn yourself in. It could have been to try to break you. You showed a fair amount of life and spirit when you escaped, and that's the only way to put it. You escaped. You showed a mind of your own, and those people don't like that. They want everyone to walk the line. They tell you what to think, what to eat, what to wear, where to work, and on and on." He nodded toward Moses. "When you took that boy and ran that was you thinking for yourself." He paused a second. "They don't like that."

"But The Group loves us and cares for us," Way said. "It gives us everything we need. I wouldn't have anything if it wasn't for The Group. The Group knows what's best for me, for everyone."

"Son," Jack adjusted his cap, then looped a thumb around his overall strap, "sounds to me like this here Group wants to take the place of the good Lord. Everything you just said is things he does for us."

Abe's fists were clenched. "How can you be so stupid? Can't you see it?"

"Okay, a little harsh there," Allen said. He smiled. "Some of us still need a little work on letting the Lord shine through us even though we've had nothing but him for most of our lives," he gestured toward Abe, "or even all our lives in some cases."

Mom stepped in the midst of the men and patted Way's back. "Forgive my boy. He's rough as a cob, but he does have his good points." She narrowed her eyes and looked at Abe while still speaking to Way. "I'm afraid you just haven't got to see much of them yet."

Way dropped his gaze to the cave floor. "Thank you. That's all right." He looked back to Mom. "What happened? The grand matron said you and the offspring, uh, Moses, were captured, that he had been extinguished and you were awaiting your opportunity to join the World Community."

Peter broke in, a finger in the air. "Minor correction, the lady said Mom was in her cell and was basically going to be given the chance to turn her back on the Lord."

Shaking her head, Mom took a deep breath. "We was all here waiting on you all to get back, and we heard a bunch of commotion outside. Them Corpsmen of yours are a noisy lot. They couldn't sneak up on a deaf, blind man, but I'm afraid we'd let our guard down for some reason. We should've knowed they'd be around. Anyways, we heard them coming, so we all started stirring. They were saying things to where we knew they knew we were here, and there wasn't going to be no getting away. We had too many people to gather up in too short of a time." By then, Mom gestured to help tell the story. "Our first thought was to take care of the baby." Mom's voice cracked. A tear rolled down her wrinkled cheek. She took in a breath. She wiped the tear away, but another followed. Then another. She sniffled. "We knew we had to save that baby." She rubbed Moses's cheek and smiled. "We knew we had to save that baby." She took in another breath and looked to the cave top. Her chin quivered. "Then someone says, 'Save Mom. Get Mom out of here.' I argued with them, best I could with them Corpsmen traipsing around outside. I tried to get them to send out some of the younger mamas or some of the teenagers, or the men, or anyone. They wouldn't do it, though. It was, 'No, Mom. It needs to be you.' 'No, Mom. We got to get you out of here.' 'No, Mom. You're the best one for the job.' They gave me the baby and was pushing me out the back entrance no matter how much I fussed and carried on. So there me and him was, heading out the back about the time them Corpsmen was busting in the front. We got outside just in the nick of time, and I did my level best to keep us hid while them Corpsmen swarmed all over."

"What then?" Peter asked.

Mom ran a sleeve across her forehead. "It was terrible. I didn't have time to get far away, so the baby and me hid in the brush yonder," she nodded toward the outside, "and I kept both of us as quiet as I could. Thank God, he's a well-mannered baby. If I'd ever tried to do that with Abraham, he'd have squawlered all over the place."

Peter looked Abe over from head to toe and nodded. "I can see that."

Mom continued. "So me and the baby were in the brush. Them men dragged our people out of the cave. They hit them with billy clubs and rifle stocks. They pushed them. They kept asking where the baby was, but none of our people would talk." Eyes glistening, she looked at Peter. "I was so proud of our people, all of them, young and old. They didn't give in to the beating. They prayed, and they encouraged each other. The more they did that, the rougher those men got, but our people didn't give in." She put her palm to her chest. "It hurt me like you wouldn't believe, but I was so proud. I wanted so bad to come out of those bushes, but I had to take care of this little fellow." She patted Moses on the head. He giggled. Mom smiled. "There was no way those men was getting him as long as I had anything to say about it."

Way had never cried that he could remember, but now tears came. He swallowed hard. "Thank you, uh, Mom, for what you did." He cleared away the tears. "People in the city just wouldn't have done something like that. They would never help a complete stranger like that." He looked around at the entire group. "All of you, you don't know me," he raised Moses slightly, "and you don't know him, but you're risking your lives for us. People in the city just don't do that. In fact, if any of them had seen us trying to get away they would have stopped us. They would have turned us in. They would have done everything they could to help the Corpsmen catch us."

Abe shifted his weight. He looked everywhere, except directly into Way's eyes. "Man, I'm sorry." He took a deep breath and exhaled sharply. "I, I don't know. I'm just sorry. I've been a total jerk to you. Somehow, it all just hit me. You're just trying to save your boy. You talk about us risking our lives, well, you risked yours for him. The way it appears you was brung up, the easiest, most likely thing for you to do would've been to just let them take him and do their thing." He pursed his lips. "You got some gumption." He reached out to Way. "Please forgive me. I hope you can forgive me and we can go on from here."

Way narrowed his eyes and drew in his chin.

"You take hold of it and shake it, bud," Allen said. "Like this." He shook Abe's hand. "It's a good thing."

Way warily reached out to Abe. Smiling, Abe grabbed Way's hand and gave it a good, firm shake. Way felt like his fingers were being crushed.

Allen laughed. "There you go. That's it."

Abe released his grip. "I'll try to do better. Like Mom said, I'm rough as a cob. Maybe it'd be different if I hadn't growed up out here in the woods and had been able to live what these guys say had been a normal life before things fell apart."

"'Normal'? 'Things fell apart'?" Way said.

"Yeah, well—" Peter started but was interrupted by Jack snapping his fingers for Shamus to go to his side.

Jack rubbed the scruff of Shamus's neck, but cast a wary glance toward the opening. "Uh, Pete, before you go into all that, don't you think we should be on the move? Them thugs could come back any second and we're sitting ducks in here."

"Let them come." Allen squared his shoulders and set his jaw. "I'm ready to die here and now."

Jack tugged at the bill of his cap. He stroked his beard. "Well, if you're talking about the spiritual sense, I'm just as ready to die as the next fellow. If you're talking about the physical sense, I'd like to hang on for a while and see what we can do. I'm ready to die, I just don't see no sense in rushing it."

"Jack has a point." Peter smiled. "Let's gather up what we can and hit the road."

"What should we get, Brother Peter?" Mom asked.

"Well, I think the fishing pole will come in handy. After that, it's kind of like my daddy used to say his managers would tell him when he ordered stuff for the store, order enough but not too much." Peter winked at Mom. "Let's take enough, but not too much."

Mom pshawed, waved at him, and gathered supplies.

Jack stroked his beard. "Say, Pete, I never knowed, what kind of living did your daddy make?"

"Well," Peter continued gathering supplies, "of course, I was a kid, but from what I gathered, he did pretty good for that time and where we lived. I think he made around twenty-two dollars an hour there at the end."

Jack nodded thoughtfully. "Twenty-two dollars an hour? Let's see, twenty-two dollars an hour times forty hours a week times fifty-two weeks a year, that's forty-five thousand, seven hundred and sixty dollars a year. You're right, not bad for that time and place."

Peter exhaled. "It amazes me how you figure stuff like that so fast. How do you do that?"

Jack waved his fingers beside his head. "I don't know. Math just kinda happens up here."

Chapter 6—Sacrifice

W ay and the others had been on the trail about half an hour and travelled a couple of miles, when they stopped to allow Mom to take a breather.

Way laid down the items he'd carried. He stood straight. "Allen, could you help me with this thing?" He motioned to the sheet they had converted into a baby sling to carry Moses on his back.

Allen lifted Moses out of the carrier and set him on the ground. "It might do you good to stretch your legs, little fellow."

Way stretched and turned from one side to the other, thankful to have the load off his back even if only for a few minutes. "Peter, back at the cave, I believe you were going to say something about something falling apart."

While the others, except Moses, sat, Peter paced about the small clearing. Every few seconds, he would peer into the woods or look to the sky. Every once in a while he cocked his head to one side or the other, as if having heard something that he wanted to give a better listen. "Yeah, it was a lot different when I was a kid. What year is it now?"

Those who had been in the woods mumbled about not knowing.

"It's Group Year 28," Way said.

Abe curled his nose. "Group Year 28? What in the world?"

Way shrugged. "I don't know, just Group Year 28."

Peter stopped pacing and faced Way. "That's what they call it now?"

Way exhaled. "It's what they've called it all my life."

"How old are you?" Peter asked.

"Twenty-four."

Peter rubbed his chin. "If all this Group Year business started twenty-eight years ago, that must've not been long after those of us who were in the city left. So I must be about forty-two."

"And I'd be about seventy." Mom pointed a shaky, crooked finger at Abe. "And you'd be about twenty-six because it was a couple of years after we came out here that you was born."

Abe pursed his lips and nodded.

Peter walked again. "That still doesn't tell us exactly what year it is, but at least we're close. I take it once this Group came into power they did away with years as we know them and started their own thing."

"That's a safe bet." Jack patted the panting Shamus's head. "They did their own thing in a lot of ways."

"And ruined the world in the process," Mom said.

"Yep." Peter paced from one side of the clearing to the other. "They sure did."

"What was it like before The Group?" Way let Moses take hold of his finger.

Peter pulled his pants up a bit. "There used to be freedom, more or less, in America, at least."

"America? What?" Way asked.

The adults stopped and stared at Way.

Way shifted his weight and scooted back a few inches. "What? What did I do? What's America?"

Jack took off his cap and rubbed his hair. "Well, I'll be ..."

Abe looked to the sky. "Lord, please help me."

"You all don't be hard on him." Mom rushed to Way's aid. "He don't know no better."

Peter resumed pacing. "Okay, this may be even more of a job than I thought." He stopped and turned to Way. "Back before your Group the world had countries. America was one of them. Among other things, it was known as 'the land of the free and the home of the brave' to quote the national anthem. Freedoms shrunk as time went on, but you were basically free to speak your mind, pursue the line of work that interested you, hunt, fish, create."

Jack put his cap back on and pulled it down snug. "It was a pretty good place for the most part. That was back when men was men and women was women, and that was a pretty good arrangement."

"Quoting Bugs Bunny cartoons again, Jack?" Peter said.

Jack smiled. "You recognize that, huh? Now those was some classics."

Allen cleared his throat. "Anyway, haven't you ever heard of America, bud?"

Way leaned in like he had a secret to tell, looking left to right and back again, "I heard a little about something that may be what you're talking about, but it's against The Group to talk about anything that happened before The Group came into power. It's as big an offense as all of you commit by saying your form of Jesus is the only way."

Peter nodded. "That's the way those things go. A person or group of people come into power—" He stopped and cocked his head to the side. He looked to the sky. "Everyone in the bushes! Now!"

All but Way and Moses scattered. It was as if Way was glued down by indecision. Abe went back, scooped Moses up, grabbed Way by the shirt collar, and yanked. Way came out of his stupor and made it behind a fallen tree and under a bush just as a drone flew overhead and fired.

Way heard another drone approaching.

Abe gave Moses to Way. "Lay on top of your boy!"

Way did as he was told.

Abe laid on top of Way. "I'll cover you! Just be sure to keep yourself up good enough that we don't squash your boy!"

Shots from the second drone zipped through trees and leaves and bushes with rapid succession. They were coming faster than the night Way escaped.

A third drone flew over firing more shots than Way could hope to count. Way dug his face into a pile of wet, dead leaves, but made sure to give Moses room to breathe.

Among the zipping and pinging of bullets there was a dull thud. Abe jerked and groaned.

Way craned his neck trying to see Abe. "What's wrong? Are you all right?"

Abe winced and wriggled. "I ... I don't think so."

Drones continued to fire.

Way tried to crawl from under Abe. "Let me get help. I'll get Peter."

"No." Abe closed his eyes and took in a halting breath. He kept Way under him. "It's no use. It wouldn't ... do ... any good."

Way felt sweat from Abe's forehead drip onto his cheek. "I have to do something."

"Stay here ... and take care ... of your boy. That's what ... you can do."

"But—"

"Shh." Abe interrupted. He blinked and took a deep breath. His lips smacked as he began to speak. "Another thing you ...can ... do ...."

"Yes. Go on."

"Please ... forgive. I ... was ... awful ... to you."

Way flinched as a flurry of bullets hit inches from them. "Don't worry about it. I brought a lot of trouble on all of you. I'm the one who should ask to be forgiven."

Abe coughed. "No. You, please ... forgive me."

"Yes, I forgive you, but why did you do this for us?"

Smiling, Abe nodded. "Thank ... you. I done it ... because you ... wasn't ready." He strained and looked to the blue sky. "And ... Lord ... you, too. Please forgive ... me." Abe went limp.

Way was desperate to get out from under Abe's body, but drones still flew overhead and sprayed their projectiles. Moses squirmed and strained against Way's weight.

None of the rebels made a sound. Way wondered if any of the others survived the onslaught.

With a final burst, the drones rained hundreds of bullets to the ground. Abe's body jarred a couple of times, apparently taking hits. Way curled into the position he normally assumed to go to sleep and pulled Moses yet closer. Way watched his fingers. He'd never seen them shake like that. He thought of Grand Matron Filleen Tannon's lilting voice reading her nightly Encouragement. "I serve The Group. The Group knows best. The Group has my best interests in mind. I am nothing without The Group. The Group takes care of me. The Group loves me. The Group is all I need. The Group has all I need."

The drones whirred away. Several seconds passed. Probably a minute.

"I'm afraid we're the only ones who made it, boy," Way said to Moses, who showed he was more than ready to get out from under Way. "I don't know what to do. We might have to go back to the city. I don't think we can make it out here."

"Hey, everyone." It was Peter. "I think it's safe to come out. Mom. Jack. Everyone. Is everyone all right?"

Way heard the others stir and come out from their hiding places. Holding Moses, he crawled from under Abe's body. He leaned heavy on the dead tree and stood. His legs wobbled. He saw the others walking to the clearing.

Mom shuffled through a patch of knee-high wildflowers. She took stock as her eyes moved from one man to the other. "My boy. Where's my boy? Where's Abraham?"

Way knew, but couldn't respond.

Peter and Allen moved to Mom's side.

Peter took hold of Mom. "It's all right, Mom. We'll find him."

"Don't anyone know where Abe is?" Jack asked.

After a few seconds of calling Abe's name and scanning the trees and bushes around the clearing, the others looked to Way.

Way lowered his head. He pointed toward the ground to his right. "I'm … sorry. I couldn't … speak. I couldn't … say it."

"Is he …?" Peter couldn't bring himself to finish the question. "Is he …?"

Head hanging, Way nodded. "I'm…sorry, Mom. He's… extinguished."

Mom crumpled to the ground out of Peter's and Allen's grip. She wailed. "My boy! Oh, my boy! Why did it have to be him? Why couldn't it have been me?"

Peter knelt beside Mom and pulled her close. "Go ahead, Mom. Go ahead."

Mom raised her head. She sniffled. "Why, Brother Peter? He was a good boy. He had some rough edges, but he was good at heart."

"Would you?" Way held Moses toward Jack.

Jack's eyes grew big, but he took Moses.

Way called Allen to the side and leaned in to him. "He didn't have to be extinguished."

Allen furrowed his brow. "What do you mean? What are you talking about?"

Way cast an uneasy glance toward Mom. "Abe. Abe didn't have to be extinguished. He was protecting Moses and me. He laid on top of us to shield us."

"Wow." Allen raised his fingers to his mouth. "Wow." He nodded toward Mom. "I think you should tell her."

"But what if it upsets her? What if she blames me? After all, it was my fault."

Allen pressed on Way's back. "No, bud. It wasn't your fault. Abe did what he felt he needed to do. It was his choice. If there's any fault, it's that Group bunch. That's who's at fault. You tell Mom. You tell her. She won't be upset at you. You want to see a Christian woman? You tell Mom and see what happens."

Way covered the distance to Mom and Peter with hesitant steps. He knelt beside Mom. "Madam, Mom, I need to tell you something."

Mom composed herself. "Yes, son. What is it?"

Way motioned toward the log that laid between them and Abe's body. "I'm sorry about your son, but there's something Allen thinks you should know."

"Yes?"

"He …, he was extinguished—"

Mom stopped Way. "He was killed, son. He's dead, not extinguished. He was killed, not extinguished. We need to call it what it is."

Although she corrected him, Mom said the words in a tone Way had never heard. He had never seen a look like the look Mom gave him. Resting on his knees, Way shifted his weight from one to the other. He pretended something in the woods caught his attention.

After a few seconds, he lowered his gaze and took an interest in his fidgeting fingers. "Yes, madam. You see, Abe was … killed … protecting Moses and me."

Mom gasped.

Way continued. "He had me lay on top of Moses, and he laid on me. He shielded us. If not for him, I would have been extinguished … killed."

A tear rolled down Mom's cheek and into a wrinkle. Mom sniffled and wiped her sleeve across her nose. Smiling, she nodded. "That boy. He always was full of surprises. Thank you for telling me, son. It's good to know he gave his life doing something worthwhile." Mom made a move to stand, and Peter helped her to her feet. She gripped Way's shoulder. "Now, you need to make it worthwhile. You need to make it count."

"Yes, madam."

"Well," Jack rifled through his backpack, "not to sound crass, but we need to bury Abe and get out of here. Them thugs or some of them flying machine guns could show up any time. We need to get a move on." He pulled out a green shovel like the ones Way had seen Corpsmen carry at times.

"We can't," Mom said. "Like you said some of them government men could show up any second. Much as I love the boy, we can't take time to bury him. We need to move. I insist."

"Now, Mom," Peter said, "we need to give him a proper burial, say a few words over him."

Mom held up a craggy finger. "Now, Brother Peter, you know as well as I do, that ain't him over there. That's just an old house. A shell. The real him ain't there no more. The real him is in the presence of the Lord."

Way curled his upper lip. "What?"

"But, Mom, don't you want to give him a final resting place?" Jack asked, ignoring Way's question.

Allen put an arm around Way's shoulder. He held a shovel in his other hand. "There's a lot going on you don't understand. I'll try to help. The Bible says to be absent from the body is to be present with the Lord. It also says it is appointed to man to die one time and then the judgment."

"You people think Abe is still alive somewhere?" Way pointed nowhere particular as he spoke.

"I believe that as much as I believe you're standing right here with me," Allen said.

Way nodded. "Interesting."

Allen smiled. "You bet it is." He made a sweeping motion. "There is something more than all this, than this life. The Lord makes this world better for us, more tolerable, but he also has something waiting for us in Heaven and eternity. What He has for us then and there is much greater than anything we can imagine."

"The Group allows various beliefs, but what you're talking about, I don't believe I've heard before."

Allen kept smiling. "Yeah, it seems that Group bunch tells you a lot of things. Remember, they also told you Mom and your boy were captured and that he was already dead." He pointed to Moses playing in the dirt. "He looks fine to me."

"All right, everybody, let's get going." Peter slung his pack on his back. "Mom's pretty insistent that we move on, and she's the one with the most stake in this, so let's go." He nodded at Mom and smiled.

"Thank you," Mom said. "I'd hate for them government men to catch us standing around Abe's shell. I'd never forgive myself if I caused you boys to get caught over someone who's not even there anymore."

"We'll talk more later, bud. Looks like we're heading out." Allen folded his shovel and put it back in his pack.

"Sure. Sounds fine." Way rigged his carrier for Moses and put the boy on his back.

Jack tugged at the bill of his cap. "Pete, what you reckon we need to do?"

Peter studied the portion of the sky he could see through the treetops. He clicked his lips. "You know more than me, but my idea would be to go deeper in the woods. I believe the farther we get from the city, the less interested they're going to be in tracking us down."

"Great minds do think alike." Jack removed his cap, rolled the bill and slapped the cap against his thigh. Dust particles floated. "That's what I was thinking."

Allen looked to the sky, squinting against the sun. "It must be about midday. When and what we going to eat?"

Jack put on his cap. He rubbed Shamus's head. "Up to Pete and Mom, but I'd say we skedaddle on away from here and find a place to settle for a few hours, then I'll go out and rustle up something."

Mom nodded.

"Sounds good," Peter said. "The more we can come up with along the trail, the better."

A few hours and several miles later, the travelers found a place to rest for the night.

Jack worked to start a fire. Peter gathered twigs and branches to feed it. Mom tended to Moses, who was glad to be free of the carrier. Allen put together a lean-to. Way didn't know what to do and stayed close to Allen. Every once in a while Allen gave Way a simple task.

"Get that thing blazing, Brother Jack." Mom hugged herself and shivered.

Peter wiped sweat from his forehead. "It must be a hundred degrees, Mom."

Mom still hugged herself. "Yeah, but the sun will go down soon, and there may be a nip in the air tonight. You know how I hate to be cold."

"Oh, I know." Peter chuckled.

Sparks flew, and a tiny flame sprouted from the sticks and dead brush Jack worked with. "Hoo-hoo! There we go! That's what we wanted to see." Jack pointed to the sticks Peter carried into the campsite. "Feed that thing, Pete. It needs fuel, got to eat."

Peter dumped the small limbs and sticks near the upstart fire and fed it as Jack had said. "Good job. You're still about the best fire starter I ever saw."

"'About the best'?" Jack grunted. "If I'm only 'about the best,' I'd say I have some work to do."

Smiling, Peter put a stick on the weak, but growing, fire. "Now that you got this thing going, why don't you go out and show us you're about the best hunter around?"

Jack slapped his thigh. "I reckon I'll do that." With grunts and groans, he stood. He tilted his head toward the fire. "You just keep feeding that thing and have it ready when I get back. Then I'll feed you all."

"Consider it fed." Peter threw another stick on the fire.

Allen left Way and the lean-to and went to Peter. "Not to be a pain, but are you sure it's a good idea to have a fire going? I mean, they have satellites and drones and who knows how many of those Corpsmen at their disposal."

Peter sat on his haunches, forearms resting on his knees. "I thought about it. I don't know. Maybe I just figured it doesn't matter much. They can probably zero in on us pretty good fire or no fire."

Allen leaned closer. "That's not very encouraging."

"True," Peter said. "I don't mean for it to be discouraging. It's just fact."

"What are we going to do if a whole herd of drones comes buzzing over? Or a bunch of those Corpsmen come storming in?"

Peter inhaled. "Well, it kind of goes back to the conversation you and I had. I plan to fight to the end, and take as many of their people and as much of their machinery down as I can. I don't want them taking me to the city, and if I have anything to say about it, they're not taking any of the rest of you either."

Allen stood straight. "But what about turning the other cheek and forgiveness?"

"Hmm." Peter bowed his head. He looked back up at Allen. He touched a finger to his right cheek. "I figure they got this cheek when Mama and Daddy died out here because of being driven out of the city for what they believed." He touched his finger to his left cheek. "Then, they got this cheek when they got my wife and girls. Top it off with them getting our people the other night, and now they got Abe." He tilted his head to one side. "I don't have any more cheeks to offer."

"Well, well, well, looky here!" Jack made a grand entrance into the campsite. He held two chickens and a full pouch. He plopped the chickens on a huge, flat rock. "Chickens has to be about the dumbest creatures God put on this earth. When I come up to these things they didn't run nor nothing. They was practically like, 'Here, wring my neck. Let me feed you.' Craziest thing I ever saw."

"That didn't take long. Good job, Jack," Peter said. "And what do you have in the bag?"

John Deere hat askew, Jack held the pouch open for the others to see. "Blackberries. Good, old blackberries. I don't figure we have the makings for Mom to whip us up a blackberry cobbler, but at least we can have us some fresh-off-the-vine blackberries."

Mom took the chickens. "Here. I'll take them chickens, Brother Jack. We'll get them fixed up in a jiffy."

Jack sat down the pouch and adjusted his cap. "I'll be right along to help you."

His wrist as limp as a wet sack, Way pointed after Mom and wrinkled his nose. "You're going to eat those?"

Allen slapped him on the back. "On the contrary, *we're* going to eat those."

"I don't know." Way curled his upper lip and flared a nostril. "The Group strictly forbids eating flesh because it's wrong on many levels."

With the fire going strong, Peter moved to help Mom. "I'd say starving to death is wrong on many levels, too. And I hate to tell you, but right now, you're so deep into it that eating a good chicken breast is the least of your worries."

Mom untied the pot that she carried on her pack. "Glad I decided to bring this. I thought about leaving it behind. Guess the Lord knew we'd need it." She held the pot toward Allen. "Would you please go to the creek and fill this?" She turned her attention to Peter. "Brother, I don't know that he'll want to eat a whole lot of meat the first few go 'rounds. That might be rough on his insides seeing how that Group of his didn't let him eat none before."

"True. He probably needs to take it easy on the meat the first few times." Peter poked the fire with a stick.

Way fidgeted. He scratched his face. "I don't know about eating flesh at all. The Group says it's wrong to eat the flesh of another animal. Plus, it's not good for our bodies."

Peter closed his eyes a few seconds. "Think about it. The same bunch that doesn't want you to eat these chickens was going to kill that boy of yours because his mama thought he was an inconvenience. We won't make you eat meat if you don't want to, but you chew on that thought while you're chewing on those blackberries."

Way was still. His gaze dropped. "I don't know about that. All I know is what The Group says."

"But you were willing to take that boy and run." Jack joined the conversation. He had one thumb hooked around the strap of his overalls. He touched a finger to Way's chest. "There's something in you that told you it was wrong for them to kill that boy." He touched Way's temple. "You knew it then, and you know it now." He gestured as he continued. "Now, whether you eat any of that chicken, or any other meat we come up with for that matter, is up to you. You can join in or you can do without. It's your choice. No one here is going to say you have to do one or the other. That's part of what being free and thinking for yourself is all about."

"And that's a small part of it," Peter said. "There was a time before everything fell apart that you could choose what to eat, what to wear, where to live, what kind of work to do."

"You keep saying 'before everything fell apart.' Exactly what are you talking about?"

Jack sucked in a breath. "Whew, boy, that's a can of worms right there."

Peter chuckled. "Yes, it is. You see, there was a time when America, the United States, was a free country, a person could pretty much choose what they wanted to do with their life, how they wanted to live it. As time went on, the government, what you call The Group now, I guess, got bigger and bigger and took more and more control of people's lives. Used to, the government didn't deliver three meals a day to your house, tell you what time to go to bed, what time to get up, what to wear and so on." He motioned toward Moses, playing in the dirt at Way's feet. "A baby's first birthday was a time to celebrate, not a time to decide if they lived or died."

Way knit his brows. "I can't even imagine. How did people do it? How did they survive? Now The Group takes care of us. The Group meets all our needs."

Jack snorted.

"There's an old quote." Peter put his fingers to his chin. "'A government big enough to give you everything you want is a government big enough to take from you everything you have.' I've seen that credited to President Gerald Ford. Some say Thomas Jefferson said it. Others say it was Ronald Reagan. They were also presidents. Anyway, who said it isn't really the point right now. The point is that this Group of yours gives you everything you need to live, but it also controls every aspect of your life and everyone else's lives."

Way shifted most of his weight to his right foot. "You mean people had to get their own food, shelter, and clothing?"

"Yep." Peter nodded.

"I don't know." Way widened his eyes. "Sounds scary to me."

"Scary?" Jack huffed. "Man, that's life. That's living. It's freedom, independence." He snorted and rolled his eyes. "Scary."

"Anyway," Peter said, "yeah, people got their own food, shelter, and clothing. At least, to an extent. Much as they could they chose their own career. If they didn't like the job they had, they could try to get another one." He smiled. "There were limits, of course. My dream was to play centerfield for the Yankees, and I never came close to that."

"What are the Yankees?" Way asked.

"Oh, yeah." Peter clicked his tongue. "Your Group doesn't have sports because of that winning and losing and someone getting their feelings hurt because the other guy's better."

Way nodded. "Right."

"The Yankees were a baseball team," Peter said and motioned to stop Way from speaking. "And before you asked what baseball is, like Allen told you earlier, it's a sport, a form of competition."

"Oh, The Group wouldn't like that at all," Way said.

"I didn't figure," Peter said.

"Let's show him." Jack straightened his cap and pulled it down snug.

"Show him?" Peter wrinkled his nose.

Jack gave a strong nod. "Yeah, show him." He rifled through his pack and pulled out a roll of duct tape. "Let's show him. Give him a lesson in the American Pastime."

"What are you going to do?" Allen asked.

Jack lifted the duct tape toward Allen. "Why, I'm going to make a baseball."

"With that?" Allen said.

"Oh, yeah." Jack eyed the tape like a father admiring a newborn son. "You've seen what we can do with this stuff. Why, give me some of this, some vinegar, and some baking soda and I could rule the world."

Peter grinned. "You think thirty-year-old duct tape can do the job?"

Jack blustered. "If duct tape can't do the job, the job can't be done. It don't matter how old it is."

Mom stopped tending the chicken. "That's amazing stuff. My husband used it for just about everything." She smiled. "That was his first step in just about any home repair. If the duct tape couldn't fix it, it was a serious matter."

"Amen to that." Jack unrolled a bit of the tape and turned a corner of it into itself, starting a ball. "That and baling wire helped me through many a repair back in the day."

Allen hoisted the bat he'd had with him since they left the cave. "I guess we have the bats."

Chapter 7—The Old Ballgame

After Jack rolled the tape into what would serve as a baseball, the men were ready for their game.

Jack tossed the ball of tape in the air a couple of feet and caught it. "So what'll it be, fellows? Workup or teams?"

"Let's go teams," Peter answered. "Jack, how about you and me against them? The older guys against the younger ones."

"Sounds good." Jack pretended to throw the ball.

"Oh, sure." Allen playfully poked a thumb toward Way. "You two leave me with the guy who didn't even know there was such a thing as baseball a couple of days ago."

"What can I say? He who hesitates is lost." Peter stretched and twisted from side to side.

"Or, you snooze, you lose." Jack laughed.

Allen huffed. "Right. That's all right. Way and I will show you guys how it's done." He tossed the bat to Way, who stepped away from it like it was toxic. Allen palmed his face. "Okay, I'll show Way how it's done, and then we'll show you how it's done."

A realization seemed to strike Peter. "Hey, wait a minute. Say, Mom, do you want to play?"

Mom wiped her hands on her pants. "No, thank you, Brother Peter. I did used to be quite the baseball player." She held up a finger. "Mind you, I said *baseball*, not softball. I'm afraid my baseball days are behind me. I better sit this one out and take care of the chicken and the little one."

"All right," Peter said. "Suit yourself." He gripped his right shoulder and moved it back and forth. "I hope I can do this without dislocating my shoulder. It's been several years since it last happened, but you never know."

"No worries." Jack waved. "If you dislocate it, I'm sure Mom can relocate it right up for you. She's good that way." He studied the sky to the west. "All right, fellows. Let's get this show on the road. We're burning daylight."

"First, don't you think we should take a few minutes to explain the game to my teammate?" Allen asked.

"I guess we can." Jack scoffed. "Ain't going to make no difference. We're going to thump you boys either way."

Allen grunted. "I don't know. I figure you're about like Mom, and your baseball days are behind you."

"Hmph. We'll see about that." Jack said. "I may be somewhere in the neighborhood of sixty, but I can show you a thing or two."

Allen grunted again. "Whatever." He patted Way's back. "Let's get you up to speed on baseball."

"Okay," Way said, then hesitated. "But why are you speaking so mean to each other? I thought you were friends."

"That?" Allen laughed and waved. "That's nothing. Just some playful what we call trash talk. It's all in fun."

"Aren't you afraid of hurting each other's feelings?"

"Hurt his feelings?" Allen jabbed a thumb toward Jack. "Are you serious? He doesn't have any feelings. His skin's as thick as an elephant's. He'll be all right."

Jack moved the ball of tape back and forth from one palm to the other. "You better believe I'll be all right. Ain't nothing that lunkhead can say or do that's going to hurt my feelings. Like I said, let's get this show on the road."

Over the next several minutes, Peter, Jack, and Allen explained the basics of baseball to Way with Mom throwing in an occasional point or two.

With the preliminary explanations out of the way, Allen strolled to the bare spot they used as home plate. "We'll bat first and give you old guys the courtesy of being home team."

"We don't need any charity from you whippersnappers, but all right." Jack went to the pitcher's spot.

Peter settled in a spot halfway between centerfield and leftfield. He cupped his hands around his mouth megaphone style. "Play ball!"

Way picked up the game with surprising ease. While the others traded barbs, he concentrated on catching the ball when it was hit or thrown to him, hitting it when it was pitched to him, and not falling down when he was running. The latter was something even Jack had trouble with, but that didn't stop him from mouthing.

They agreed to three innings figuring the chicken should be ready about that time. Going into the bottom of the third, Way and Allen led 11-8.

Allen stood at the pitcher's spot. "We got this. Three up and three down and we're the champs."

Jack scoffed. "More like chumps."

Allen jerked his head to one side. "Just step in there old-timer. Let's get this over with. I want to put you boys out of your misery."

"Actually, I'm up," Peter said.

"Doesn't make any difference." Allen smirked. "One old-timer's the same as another."

Peter and Jack scored two runs to make it 11-10. They had two outs, Jack was up to bat and Peter was on third.

With his left foot on the rock they used as third, Peter stepped his other foot toward home and leaned on his knee. "Come on, Jack. Knock me in."

Jack took a couple of warm-up swings. He took his stance and nodded toward Allen on the pitcher's mound. "Let's do this thing."

"Consider this thing done," Allen said. He pretended to spit in his palm, rubbed the ball, and bent over peering toward home. He nodded.

Jack connected with the pitch and knocked it down the leftfield line, barely fair. Peter scored, and Jack chugged into second base with a double. "Whoo-hoo! Here we go now!" He turned his cap backward. "Rally caps!"

The score was 11-11.

Peter picked up a bat. "Okay, fellows, if we don't score it's a tie game." He squinted skyward. "It's getting dark, and the chicken's ready."

"Oh, no, there ain't going to be no tie," Jack said. "Either we win this thing now, or we suspend the game and pick it up tomorrow in extra innings before we hit the road. Ties are for communists and sissies."

Grinning, Peter rubbed his forehead. "Oh, brother."

Peter brushed his hair from his eyes. He smiled and readied himself at home. He rested the business end of the bat on the far side of home and shifted his weight.

"Make him pitch to you, Pete!" Jack called.

At the pitcher's mound, Allen turned his attention from Peter to Jack. "Man, that must be the hundredth time you've said that. Don't you have any other ways to encourage him?"

Jack clapped. "Oh, not really. That one works for me." He looked to Peter. "Make him pitch to you, Pete!" He clapped and chuckled. "There, that makes a hundred and one."

Peter stepped away from home. "That reminds me of a kid I played with when I was in Little League. He'd say that very thing. He said it so much it even got on my nerves. I'm sure it bugged the stuffing out of the teams we played."

Peter stroked the next pitch to centerfield for a hit. Way ran to retrieve it.

Head down, Jack set sail. In the two-man version they played, he had to score or he was out. He rounded third, but the turn proved too much for him. He stumbled, stumbled, stumbled. His bouncing belly did nothing to help him keep his feet.

Way reached the ball. Allen covered home.

Jack continued his stumble. He couldn't maintain his footing and fell headlong, face first toward home.

Way threw the ball. Jack landed a few feet short of home, then scrambled on all fours to touch it a fraction of a second before Allen caught the ball.

After lying at home a few seconds, Jack managed to get to his knees, held his arms straight in front of himself, and moved them away from each other. "Safe!" He plopped to the ground and tried to catch his breath. After several seconds, he managed to speak. "Chalk ... one ... up ... for ... the ...old ... guys."

Allen flung the ball of tape to the ground in mock disgust and kicked up some dust. "You old coots were lucky. You have to give us a chance to even the score somehow."

Peter ambled to home. He bent forward and leaned on his knees. "I don't know about that old coot, but I don't know that this old coot has any more sport in him. Man, that wore me out."

Wobbly legged, Way made his way from the outfield. He sat on the ground near Jack.

"Well, bud, what did you think?" Allen asked.

Way took in a deep breath. "Well, my legs shake so bad I don't think I can take another step. My arm feels like it's going to fall off. My chest is pounding, and my head throbs like I've been beat with one of those bat things you use in this game." He smiled and brushed a strand of hair from his eyes. "Other than spending time with the boy, uh, Moses, in the past year, I've never enjoyed anything more in my life."

Peter stood straight. "You mean it didn't hurt your feelings to lose?"

Moses uneasily went to Way, settled in his lap and snuggled in. Way looked toward Peter and shielded his eyes against the setting sun. "You mean, we what you call lost? Hmm. No. Doesn't bother me. Maybe it's not so bad after all. If I can ever walk again, I might want to play some more."

"You boys better get over here and grab you some chicken." Mom wiped sweat from her brow. "There's plenty to go around. Way, if you're going to eat some, you probably better not eat much since you never had meat before. Even though it's good for what ails you, it might be a touch rough on your system to start out."

Way sucked in a breath. "I don't know. The Group says—"

"Who cares what your Group says?" Jack was still lying on his belly, his cheek pressed to the ground. "They also told you sports was bad and losing was bad. You survived that. And I must say, you made a good show of yourself, held up your end of the bargain. You're out here where you can't or don't always have to go on what they say. What does Way say?"

"He's got a point there, bud," Allen said. "Of course, in the end, out here, this bunch, we also try to go on what God says."

"I'd hate to have to give this chicken to the dog," Mom said. "If you boys don't hurry, that's just what I'll do."

Jack grunted as he rose from laying on his belly to sitting. Allen and Peter walked gingerly to the fire, where the chickens simmered.

Way walked, too, but his legs shook so bad he wasn't sure he would make it. "The Group requires us to do twenty minutes of physical activity a day, but it didn't prepare me for all this running."

Moses toddled alongside Way.

Jack grunted more as he stood. He gripped his lower back and walked with a stoop. He groaned. "Oh, my sacroiliac. Anyway, there's lots of things they didn't prepare you for."

After the men, Moses, and Shamus gathered around, Mom interlocked her fingers at her stomach. "Brother Peter, would you ask the blessing?"

"Glad to, Mom." He closed his eyes, bowed his head and offered a short prayer.

Mom removed the chickens from the pot and placed them on a baby blanket she had pulled from her pack.

Way wondered how long it had been since the blanket had been washed, if ever. He thought the chicken would have been just as well off setting on the ground as on the dingy blanket. Back home, The Group picked up clothes and linens weekly for washing. In addition, workers came once a week to give the pod a thorough cleaning.

Mom tore meat from the chickens and placed the shreds on the blanket. The other men went after it, not concerned at all that Mom hadn't washed her hands. Way's stomach turned.

"Good stuff, Mom," Jack said with a mouthful of chicken.

"Thank you, Brother Jack."

"You're welcome." Jack waved a shred of chicken as he spoke. "Yes, ma'am. This here's one of the best meals out of all the meals I've ate since I been out here. Let's see." Jack closed one eye and tilted his head. "We've probably averaged a couple of meals a day every day for the twenty-eight years we been out here. That makes, um, twenty thousand, four hundred and forty meals, plus another fourteen for seven leap year days, so twenty thousand, four hundred and fifty-four meals. And this is one of the best." He winked at Mom. "Good job, Mom."

"Aw." Mom blushed. "Thank you, again, Brother Jack."

Peter smiled. "It amazes me how you come up with that stuff so fast." He snapped his fingers. "Boom. Just like that."

"I don't know." Jack put a finger to his temple. "Like I tell you, math just kinda happens up here."

Allen lifted a piece of meat Way's direction. "You don't know what you're missing. You going to get you some?"

"I don't know." The combination of the unsanitary conditions and the thought of eating flesh for the first time, going against one of The Group's strictest rules, was almost more than Way's stomach could take. He eyed the chicken. He eyed the pouch of blackberries.

"Son, I know your bunch has its rules and all, but them berries ain't going to take you far," Mom said. "You need some substance."

"She's right," Peter weighed in. "I know they have all sorts of laws and guidelines and whatnot, but out here food may get hard to come by. We can't be too picky about what we eat. Right now, we need to be thankful it's chicken. On down the road it could be dog."

"Hey, hold on there." Jack pulled Shamus close.

Peter's face reddened. "No offense, Shamus. I didn't mean you. It would never be you. That was just an example of what it could come to."

"Well," Jack blustered, "let's just be a little more careful about our examples, if you don't mind."

Peter was obviously amused by the exchange. "Anyway, okay, let's say it could be a rat or earthworms or who knows what. We'll be thankful for whatever the Lord provides, but right now, we can be just a little more thankful."

"Amen," Allen replied.

"Here, here." Jack had another mouthful of meat.

"So, what'll it be, son?" Mom asked.

Way eyed the morsel of meat Mom held. He wrinkled his nose. "I don't believe so. Thank you just the same."

"All right. It's your choice." Mom popped the meat into her mouth.

"That's okay." Allen sat, knees upraised, and fingers intertwined around them. "Out here the pickings can be mighty slim, but you do have a choice."

Peter stood and stretched. "I believe we should get a couple hours rest then do our moving while it's dark. That's probably what we should've been doing all along. I imagine it's at least a little harder for the government to find us or see us at night."

"True, Pete." Jack rubbed Shamus's head. "I was thinking the same thing."

Way swallowed a blackberry. He held up a finger. "Just a minute, please. You've mentioned how things fell apart, but haven't told me what happened. It seems things keep coming up."

Peter looked around the site, apparently sizing up what he felt needed to be done. He relaxed his stance and pursed his lips. "All right. This seems to be about as good a time as any." He sat on a fallen tree. He rubbed his palms together, then rubbed them on his thighs. "Now, I'm going to give this to you as I saw it through the eyes of a twelve- to fourteen-year-old boy. Things had been going on for years, decades even, then it got hot and heavy over that last couple of years. I'm going to let you know how it all happened in my world." He motioned in a half-circle taking in Mom, Jack, and Allen. "These guys will have different perspectives. Mom and Jack were full-grown adults when it all took place so they probably know more of what went wrong than I do. They got to see things headed this way for a longer time. Allen, well, he's a fair number of years younger than me, so he was even more just along for the ride than I was. He lived a lot of it, he just didn't know it."

Allen sat cross-legged on the ground a few feet from Peter. "That pretty well sums it up."

Way swept Moses up, sat beside Allen, and held Moses on his lap. "All right. What happened?"

Peter waved. "Like I said, this is from kid's perspective, so take it for what it's worth."

"Give it to him, Pete." Jack patted Shamus on the head. "It'll be worth more than he could ever get from that Group bunch of his."

"Amen." Mom nodded.

Peter smiled. He took in a deep breath. "Okay. Here goes. I won't give you the whole two-hundred-and-fifty-plus-year history of the United States, but I'll say it was a great country." He nodded toward Way, seeming to know what Way was thinking. "Back when we had countries, before everything fell apart. People said it was the greatest country in history. You could try to be just about anything you wanted, and if you had what it took and had enough gumption, you had a decent shot to make it. If you wanted to start a business, you could start a business. People had what they called freedom, freedom of speech, freedom of religion, freedom to own guns, freedom to believe pretty much whatever they wanted to believe."

Way held up a finger. "What's a business?"

Jack groaned, but caught himself. "Oops, sorry. I guess since Abe ain't here to show disgust, I felt the need to."

"Now, Brother Jack, we're trying to help the boy," Mom said.

Peter tugged at his shirt, untucking a bit of it. "That's right, Brother Jack. We're trying to help the boy. Thank you, Mom."

"You're quite welcome."

"Anyway, back to your question." Peter turned his attention to Way. "A business is ..., well, a business ..., hmm." He rubbed his chin. "Okay, here you go. A business is when I offer you something, a product, for instance, or a service." He tugged at his shirt again. "Let's say you wanted to buy this shirt. You would give me money for it. You would take it and it would be yours. If I had dozens or hundreds or even thousands of shirts and sold them to you and lots of others, that would be a business basically." He studied Way a few seconds, apparently to see if his words registered. "My shirt, that's a product. I can also offer you a service. Let's say your grass needs cut, and you don't have time to do it. You can pay me, give me money, and I will do it for you."

Way held up a finger again. "I don't know money. I don't understand that. And why would I want your shirt? I told you The Group gives me clothes every year. The Group also sends the cutters to take care of the grass around my pod, so there would be no need for me to give you this, what you call money, to cut the grass. The Group takes care of that. The Group gives me all I need."

"They may seem to *give* you all you need," Allen replied, "but it's not giving at all. They've taken everything from you and everyone else." He shut his eyes and inhaled. He released the breath. "Sorry, Peter, you can go ahead."

Peter waved off Allen's apology. "No problem. This doesn't have to be a one-man lesson. Anyway, we used to have freedom to make our own choices. We could even choose what to eat for our meals."

Way's eyes widened. "Really?"

"Yep. If you wanted meat, you ate meat. You wanted salad, you ate salad. You were responsible for what you ate."

"The Group takes care of that for us. The Group knows what's best, knows what we need to be healthy and to operate at our best."

"I get that." Peter couldn't hide a tinge of frustration. "We're trying to show you there's another way. At least there used to be. Now, can I go on?"

Way offered a quick shrug. He let Moses hold his index finger. "Sure."

Peter sighed. "I'll try to get right to it, to when everything fell apart. Issues had started long before, even forty, fifty, sixty years before, with people seeing and saying everything they thought was wrong with America, wanting America to be like other countries."

"Other countries that weren't as good or as strong as America, mind you," Jack chimed in.

"Amen," Mom said.

"It came to the point that everything you saw on the regular news or read in most newspapers—" he stopped himself and looked at Way. "I realize you don't know what a newspaper is. It was one form of receiving news." He spread his arms. "It was printed on paper about yay big. You bought it, and you could read what was going on in your town or even around the world.

"Anyway, just about everything you saw on television, or your computer or read in the newspaper was telling you something that was wrong with America. It got so people rioted against the government, politicians, the police, businesses, just about anyone or anything. They destroyed property and burned flags, cars, buildings: about anything they could light a match to. After that, the regular news was all about everything that was wrong with those people and institutions that were being protested against. That was one thing about the news people, they could tell you what they wanted you to hear. They could write what they wanted you to read."

Jack rubbed Shamus's side. "Pretty much what your Group does now, I'm sure. They tell you what they want you to hear, write what they want you to read."

"Hmm." Way furrowed his brow.

"I'd say that hits it about right." Peter paced in front of the others. "As time went along, things got pretty chaotic. Other countries were acting up, testing weapons they threatened to use against us and our allies; the media telling people everything that was wrong with us and our way of life, whether it was true or not. After a couple years of that and with powerful people working behind the scene, someone came out with this plan. Remember, I was only fourteen or so, but the way it seemed to me the idea was that the responsibility of electing leaders should be taken from the people and given to," and at that he made quote marks with his fingers, "'those who knew better.' They said elections should be left to people who had the best interests of the people at heart. Sound familiar?"

Way's eyes widened. "That's what The Group does."

Jack stopped petting Shamus and raised a finger. "Uh, that's what that Group *says*."

Peter stroked his beard and continued pacing. "I thought you might recognize that. That was the seed that your Group came from. They said these people would take care of us. They would free us from the burden of needing to pay attention to politics, free us from the burden of having to worry about who to elect. They would do the choosing for us. Funny thing is, the people who said they would do the electing for us were people who had been elected themselves."

"How are leaders chosen now, bud?" Allen held out a stick to Moses for a small game of tug-of-war.

"Well," Way knit his brow, and his eyes shifted from side to side. "Actually, I don't really know. People try to rise up in The Group's ranks and then every few years, they tell us who our new leader is. They have people that choose all leaders from the floor my pod is on all the way to grand patron or grand matron."

Jack tilted his head to one side. "And you don't see a problem with that?"

Way expelled a quick breath. "Well, no. I mean, I don't have to worry about anything. The Group gives me food, clothing, a task, tells me who my leaders are."

"Not to be difficult," Allen said, "but if you don't have anything to worry about, why are you out here in the woods with us?"

"Well, uh …," Way's voice trailed off. He blinked. "You see, I, uh, well, the offspring, er, Moses, I told you they were going to extinguish him."

"So your son had something to worry about?" Peter asked and gestured for Way to respond.

"Yes, I guess. I mean, they were going to extinguish him."

Peter put his foot on a fallen tree and rested his elbows on his upraised knee. "If your son wasn't safe from this Group, what makes you so sure you are?"

Way brushed beads of sweat from his forehead.

"He's a year old." Peter stood straight. "He needs protection, not someone deciding they want to get rid of him because he's an inconvenience or nuisance."

Way pulled Moses close. "Well, Luka, my domestic partner, had that privilege. The Group says the mother can decide."

"Them thugs, from the ones chasing us all the way up to that old heifer grand matron lady, are playing God." Mom pointed that well-aged finger. If it had been a gun, Way would have got it between the eyes. "No matter what they say, it ain't right to kill an innocent baby. They can take it and twist it however they want, but it ain't right. In your heart of hearts, even you know that. Even though they spent your whole life teaching you otherwise, when it came down to it, you knew that baby should be allowed to live."

Way hung his head. "Now I'm not so sure that was a good idea. I mean, look at us, out here in the woods. Corpsmen could come any second. I've endangered you. I've endangered myself."

"Whoa, whoa, whoa." Mom waved. "You've endangered yourself? Son, what you did is put your child above yourself, which is what a parent should do. Them thugs got it all wrong. Once you're a parent, it ain't about what's easy for you or what's best for you. First, you serve God. After that you take care of your family. Your job is to put that baby's well-being above your own. You did the right thing taking off with that boy." With upraised palms, she scoured the treetops. "And, yes, you're in danger. We're in danger, and your boy is in danger. We're all out here in the woods. Well, sometimes doing the right thing can leave you out in the woods, but it's still the right thing."

Peter clicked his tongue. "Well said."

"Amen," Jack said.

Peter rubbed his palms together. "Back to when it all fell apart. Apparently, the beginning of this Group thing came into play. It came out that they were going to relieve the people of the burden of choosing their leader." He hitched his thumbs in his belt loops. "My folks, especially my dad, had a big problem with that. A lot of people had a big problem with it. The leaders knew people would have a big problem with it. There was going to be an uprising like there hadn't been since the Revolution." He stopped and eyed Way. "And I know you don't know what the American Revolution was. Basically, it was when America won its freedom from England. Anyway, they knew there would be a battle, so, about half a minute after it came out that the leaders would choose our officials, it came out that they were taking guns from private citizens. They said the only people who needed weapons were law enforcement officers and military personnel."

Jack clicked his tongue. "Remember it like it was yesterday."

"Me, too." Peter jabbed a thumb upward. "Dad went through the roof. When it came to that, he knew it was time to get out of town. Nobody, and I mean nobody, was taking his guns. So we loaded up and high-tailed it out here into the woods. Mom and Dad passed away long ago, and I've been out here ever since."

"Those were dark days." Mom clasped her fingers at her waist. "My husband reacted a lot like you said your daddy did. He knew things were going from bad to worse, and he wanted to get as far from it as he could."

Way stroked Moses's hair. "I don't understand. What was wrong with them choosing your officials? What was wrong with them taking weapons? The Corpsmen are the only ones who need weapons. They have to enforce the rules. There's no reason for anyone else to have a weapon."

Jack grumbled. "That's what they want people to think. Regular people needed, need, guns to protect themselves from criminals and, in a worst-case scenario, an outlaw state. Without guns, people are at the mercy of hooligans and thugs of every stripe. Oh, don't get me started."

Peter sat next to Way. "You see, you don't have any clue about freedom. The government picking your clothes and fixing your meals isn't freedom. The government providing you with a roof over your head and a task isn't freedom. The government providing for even the possibility of Moses here being killed on his first birthday sure isn't freedom." He fidgeted with his earlobe. "You have no idea what freedom is. Why, by the time I came along, freedom wasn't even what it had been when my dad was a boy, or when his dad was a boy or his dad was a boy and so on."

"I … I just don't get it." Way moved one way and the other to situate Moses on his lap.

"I definitely understand that." Peter sat straight and twisted his shoulders, apparently working out some kinks. "We've given you a lot to digest." He held up a finger. "Just remember, we're trying to help you while that Group bunch is trying to capture you and take you and your boy into custody so he can be killed and they can do who knows what to you." He cocked his head to the side. "Remember that good." He stood and rubbed his palms down his pant legs. "Well, all, it's late, getting dark. What say we get a couple hours sleep and then hit the trail through the night?"

"Sounds like a winner, boss man," Jack said.

Allen laid down and interlocked his fingers under his head. "I'll go for that."

Mom went to Way and reached down to Moses, who reached up to her. "Son, I'll take this little fellow, and you can get you some sleep."

"Thank you, uh, Mom." Uneasy, Way hung his head.

Mom put a finger to Moses's slobbery chin. "You're quite welcome. I'm glad to do it."

Sore from the baseball game, Way grunted as he laid down. "That's very kind of you. All of you have been good to me."

Allen finished a yawn. "I'm sure you don't understand it, but it's what the Lord would have us do. And not only that, we do it because we want to. We like you."

Way nestled back and forth making a sleeping spot. He stopped. "You like me? No one, not even Luka, ever told me they liked me."

"Well, bud," Allen responded, "it seems you're in a whole new world in more ways than one."

Mom rested Moses on her hip. And gently rocked him side to side. "Brother Peter, you go on to sleep. I'll get the baby to sleep and keep watch for a little while."

"You sure, Mom?" Peter said. "We did a lot of walking today. You chased after the baby *and* fixed the chicken while we played ball. You put in a hard day."

Mom waved him off. "It was nothing. Like I said, you get some sleep. I can keep watch. I can say, 'Somebody's coming,' just as good as any of the rest of you."

Peter smiled. "All right. Have it your way. I'm pretty sure there's no point arguing with you."

"It's never worked for anyone else. I can't see no reason why it'd work for you now." Mom returned the smile. With that, she turned and started pacing around the camp, humming softly to Moses.

Chapter 8—Newcomers

A few hours later, Way awoke to Allen attempting to wake Peter. Mom had apparently laid the sleeping Moses down and turned the night watch duties to Allen. Chirping crickets and croaking tree frogs dominated the night sounds.

"Peter."

Way stirred, halfway between sleep and wake.

"Peter."

Way saw Allen kneeling beside Peter.

Peter rose, resting on one elbow. "What is it?"

"I heard something," Allen said.

That was enough to get Peter fully awake. He sat and cocked his head to the side, listening. "What did you hear? Where was it?"

"I thought I heard leaves crunching and someone talking. It was over there." Allen motioned to the east.

Peter made eye contact with Way, seeing he was awake. He poked Allen. "Wake up Mom and Jack." He urged Allen into action with a slight nudge and picked up one of the baseball bats. He tossed it to Way's side and grabbed another one for himself. "You did a good job with one of these in our ballgame. I hope you can do the same with a person."

"Hello, the camp," a man called from the woods.

Way scooped up Moses and joined the others huddling around Peter.

"Don't worry," the man said. "We're friendlies. If we wanted to harm you we surely wouldn't have been as noisy as a herd of stampeding elephants."

"Who are you? Where are you?" Peter said to the darkness.

"We're over here, and we haven't any firearms. All we have are a bow and some arrows, a hammer, knives, and some clubs."

"What are we going to do, Brother Peter?" Mom whispered.

Peter took in a deep breath and exhaled sharply. "Well, we might as well call them in. If they're government men, they got us anyway." He had Way give Moses to Mom and signaled for the men to take up their weapons. He faced the direction from which the voice had come. "You can come in."

Way knew if the visitors had firearms he and the others wouldn't have a chance against them.

Two men stepped into the clearing with their arms raised. Shamus growled from deep in his belly.

"Don't shoot," said one of the men. Way recognized the voice as the one who had called into the camp. "If you have guns, don't shoot. Jesus is Lord of lords and King of kings." With one finger the man pointed at himself. "I'm Thomas." He turned his finger to the other man. "This is Bart."

Peter narrowed his eyes. "Yes, Jesus is Lord of lords and King of kings. He is. He is, indeed." He took quick glances at Mom, Jack, and Allen.

Each of the men had an aluminum baseball bat strapped to his side. Thomas had a knife sheathed at his waist, and Bart had a bow looped around his torso and a quiver full of arrows on his back.

Peter tilted his head to one side and held his bat at the ready. "What brings you all around here? Is it just you two?"

Thomas relaxed his stance a bit. "We're just two guys trying to avoid those Corpsmen. Right now, we're out doing some hunting. Got to put food on the table, you know."

Peter relaxed. "Yeah, got to put food on the table."

Jack eyed the two newcomers. "There ain't no one else in your group?" He rubbed Shamus's head. Shamus growled again and the hair on his back stood.

Thomas shifted from one foot to the other. "No, sir, there ain't. Not anymore."

Allen rested the business end of his club on the ground and leaned on it. "Where you all stay?"

"The Lord has truly blessed us," Bart answered. "We, we got us a place."

Peter lowered his club and took a step back. "You all are hunting. We have some blackberries if you're interested."

"Yeah, we ain't got no meat." Jack poked his thumb toward the pile of chicken bones at the edge of camp. "These animals ate it down to the bone. I'm surprised they stopped there."

Mom gave Jack a playful smack on the back of the head as she walked past. "Hmph! You did your fair share of bone cleaning, Brother Jack." She went on to Thomas and Bart. "I'd say you two can relax." She looked back at Peter.

"Yeah, yeah." It was like Peter came out of a daze. "You can put them down." There was a slight pause. "But I would like you to free yourselves of your weapons."

"Give up our weapons?" Thomas said. "Now, wait. We gave the appropriate signal. Jesus is Lord of lords and King of kings. You seemed to be familiar with it. What more do you want?"

Peter nodded. "Yeah, you gave the signal." He glanced at Jack, then turned back to Thomas. "You gave the signal. Still, I'd feel more comfortable if you'd just give up your weapons. You know, temporarily, until we know you a little better."

"Wait, Peter." Allen stepped in. "Why should they have to give up their weapons? If they're with that Group bunch don't you think there are likely more of them in the woods just waiting to come in? Don't you think they'd have been loaded up and ready to take us without all the niceties?"

"What he says is true, brother," Thomas said. He unsheathed his knife and held it, blade pointed back at himself, toward Peter. "I'll gladly give up my weapons as a show of good faith, but if we were Corpsmen, don't you think we would have descended on you with all the resources The Group has available? And from what we hear those resources are unlimited. If we were Corpsmen don't you think we would've come in unannounced with guns blazing, as they say? From what I hear of the Corpsmen, if we were them, you would've already been dead or on your way to the city to face trial."

Peter wiped his forehead. "I reckon what you say is true. It's just that we can't be too careful."

"Oh, I know. I know. I take it that means we can keep our meager weapons." Thomas sheathed his knife and smiled.

"Yeah, you can keep your weapons."

"Good." Thomas extended his hand and walked to Peter,

Bart went to Jack and then Allen. There were handshakes and introductions all around.

Thomas squatted by the fire. "Say, uh, I know we just met, and you don't know us, and we don't know you, but we have a place, a little cabin," He jerked his head to the east. "It's back that way. You all are welcome to come and spend some time there. A day, two, you might even decide you want to call it home."

Peter scratched his head and rumpled his face. "I don't know." He eyed Way and Moses, but kept talking to Thomas. "We're kind of in a position where we really need to keep moving. We'd get pretty antsy just sitting for any length of time."

Thomas tossed some twigs on the fire and watched them burn. "That place has been good to us for a long time. It's a roof over our heads. It's out of the way. No Corpsman has been in that area for I don't know how long."

Again, Peter kept his eyes on Way and Moses, but spoke to Thomas. "It may have been good to you for a long time, but every day you're there, you're one day closer to those government thugs finding it, and they will find it. They've been especially thick out here the last couple of weeks."

"Like I said, you could give it some time. It might refresh you a bit to spend a couple of days there. We can all join together, take our turns on watch. If any Corpsmen show up we have an escape route. Just because we haven't seen any of them for a while doesn't mean we're not prepared for them."

"I say we do it," Allen said. "We're going to watch for those government men whether we're out here or in a cabin."

Peter rubbed the back of his neck. "But I'm afraid in a cabin we'll be sitting ducks or like shooting fish in a barrel. Jack?"

"Whatever you say, boss man. I see pros and cons both ways. Being able to kick my feet up and having actual doors and windows might not be an all bad thing."

"Mom? Peter asked.

Mom rubbed her palms on her pant legs. "Like Brother Jack said, I can see good and bad both ways."

"Like I mentioned," Thomas said, "if any Corpsmen show up, which they haven't for, I don't know, probably years, we do have a way out. You, we, wouldn't completely be sitting ducks as you put it." He nodded toward Way. "How about you? We haven't heard from you, brother."

The question caught Way by surprise. "I don't know." One by one he took quick studies of his new traveling partners. Peter seemed all the way on one side of the argument, Allen was all the way on the other side, and Mom and Jack were in the middle. None of them did anything to try to influence Way. "I guess I'd like to have an actual place to stay. Living in the woods isn't really for me. Maybe we can do it for a few days and then, Peter, if you still think we need to move on, we can. That's …, that's what I think, anyway. The Corpsmen seem to be able to find people out here whether they're on the move or sitting still."

Peter exhaled. He bit his lip. "Well, it looks like I'm the only one dead set against it." He pressed his lips together. "I still don't think it's a good idea, but I'll go along with all of you."

"Good choice." Smiling, Thomas stepped to Peter and patted him. "You won't be sorry."

Peter ducked his head and scratched the back of his neck. "I hope not. I'm responsible for a lot of lives here, and I don't want to blow it." He raised his head and looked Thomas in the eye. "If this goes bad and it's in any way because of you and your friend there, you're at the top of the list."

Now Thomas's smile seemed forced. He stepped back. "Whoa, hey. That sounded like a threat."

Peter cocked his head to one side. "Nah, that was truth."

Allen stepped between Peter and Thomas. "Okay. Calm down. We're going to be spending a lot of time together, we need to get along. We're all brothers and sister here, and we all have the same enemy. Let's not forget, we're on the same team."

Thomas clicked his tongue and tilted his head to one side. "Sounds good to me. Some of us have gotten off to a rocky start here. I'm willing to move past that. These are tough times for all of us. Sometimes the stress can boil over."

Peter ran his fingers through his hair. "I apologize." He motioned in a semi-circle taking in the members of his group. "These people are my family, and I'm protective of them. I don't want to see harm come to any of them."

"Understandable." Thomas gave a thumbs up. "I'm with you. I know what it's like to have people you feel responsible for. Bart and I, we used to have several people that we oversaw. Unfortunately, through one thing and another, it dwindled to just him and me."

"Now where's this mansion you was talking about?" Jack hitched a thumb around his overall strap.

"It's not exactly a mansion." Thomas snickered and fidgeted with his knife handle. "It's a little rough."

"Rough or not, I'm sure it's a mansion compared to the places we've stayed over the last several years," Allen said.

Peter surveyed the campsite. "Well, let's gather up our gear, and if it's all right with these fellows, we can head on to their place."

"Sounds good to me," Thomas said. "The sooner the better. You said you're afraid you'll be a sitting duck staying in one place, well, I feel like a sitting duck being out here in the open."

Chapter 9—The Cabin

Thomas pushed open the cabin door. "I'm home, dear." He stepped in and to the side and motioned for the others to enter. "Look what followed me home, Dad. Can I keep them?" He laughed.

Bart rolled his eyes.

From his vantage point with his back against the front wall, Way tried to see who else was in the cabin and where they were. He couldn't see anyone. The others in Way's group looked at each other, apparently as confused as he was.

His cheeks red from laughter, Thomas caught his breath. "Oh, I'm sorry. I just had to do that."

Bart stood a couple inches taller than Thomas and was more muscular. "I'm sorry, too. He just *has* to do it every time he comes through the door." It was the first thing he had said since they had been at the campsite.

Way took note of Peter, who gave the cabin a wary eye.

Jack dropped his pack, plopped down on the couch in the middle of the front room and plopped his feet onto the coffee table. He interlocked his fingers behind his head.

"Make yourself at home, Jack," Allen said.

"Ahhh, I believe I will," Jack said. "I believe I will. This is the first actual piece of sitting furniture I sat on in years. Come on, Mom. Why don't you join me? Have a seat."

Mom hesitated. She looked at Bart, then Thomas.

Thomas hung some of his gear on the wall. "It's okay, ma'am. Go ahead and sit. We do want you to make yourself at home."

Peter walked about the room, scanning from floor to ceiling. The living room and kitchen were open in one relatively big space. Peter moved into the kitchen area still scanning from floor to ceiling. He opened the cast iron wood cook stove. "Looks like it hasn't been used much lately."

"We've just been batching it." Thomas waved. "You know, catch as catch can and whatnot."

Peter closed the oven door. "I see." He went down the narrow hallway off the living room,

Way leaned forward, peering after him. Peter disappeared into a room.

"You won't find anyone back there," Thomas called. "And you won't find anything out of the ordinary either."

"Just having a little look around," Peter said. "If you ever stayed in a motel you took a little tour of the room, didn't you?"

"Of course." Thomas stood at the entrance to the hallway. "Back before, you know, before things went bad, my family stayed in new places every now and then. I'd snoop around every nook and cranny and open doors and drawers. So you go right ahead."

"I was going to."

Allen sat on the couch with Jack and Mom. Way sat Moses on the floor. Within seconds, Moses stood and was toddling about the room. Like Peter, he explored the new surroundings.

Thomas directed Way to a cushioned chair a couple of feet from the couch. "You can watch the boy from there. Don't worry about him, though. There's nothing in here he can hurt, and I doubt there's much of anything here that can hurt him."

Outside, Shamus barked several times. He pawed at the front door.

"Shamus, quiet." Jack said. "Sorry about that. He's not used to being away from me."

"Quite all right," Thomas said. "I can understand that. I had a pup that I was quite fond of before—" he stopped himself. He seemed to search the ceiling for the words. "Before things went bad."

"Not a bad setup." Peter went back into the living room. "A couple of bedrooms, a bathroom. No running water, of course, but I wasn't expecting the Waldorf Astoria." He ran his fingers through his hair. "Now, where's this secret way out if the thugs show up? We better find out now because when they show up it'll be too late."

Thomas leaned against the wall. "Don't worry about that. Bart or I will always be around. We can take you to it easy enough if or when the time comes."

Peter stood straight, squared his shoulders, tilted his head to one side, and raised an eyebrow. "You need to tell us how to get out of here if the government thugs show up. My friends and I don't know that we can count on you and Bart to come through for us in crunch time. We've been there for each other and know we can trust each other. You two, we just met. We've known you a couple of hours. We don't know how you deal with pressure, how you react when things get tough, or if you'll really even help when they show up." He motioned toward Bart. "He's a big, ol' boy and all, but I haven't heard him string three words together since you two came into our camp. I don't know that he has the vocabulary to tell us how to get to that secret way out if he has to."

Standing near the front door, Bart stiffened.

Peter rubbed his forehead and exhaled. "I just call 'em like I see 'em. You need to show us that way out."

Thomas stood straight. "All right. All right. Is he always so testy?" he asked the others.

"He's a good guy." Jack continued to rest his feet on the coffee table. "He takes good care of us and will do whatever it takes to see that we're okay."

"If you say so." Thomas trudged toward the hallway. "It's in the back bedroom. Who wants to come along?"

"Why don't we all go?" Peter said. "That way we can all get to it if need be."

Way watched as Jack and Allen fell in line behind Thomas and Peter. He followed along.

Mom waved after them. "You all go on. I'll stay here with the baby. You can tell me how to get there."

"You sure, Mom?" Peter called back.

"I'm sure. You'll be able to describe it to me just fine." Mom leaned forward and tickled Moses's chin. "Won't he, big boy?"

Thomas opened the closet door, knelt, and lifted a trapdoor. "Here you go." He led the others down the stairs into a dirt-walled tunnel. He pulled a small flashlight out of his pocket and shined it ahead.

Where walls and ceiling met, cobwebs hung almost the entire way. Water bugs scattered as the men made their way along. Crickets hopped out of the way.

"So many insects," Way said, his voice echoing through the tunnel. "I'm not used to seeing so many insects. Actually, I'm not used to seeing any insects."

"Well, be sure not to step on any of them because I'm sure that Group bunch would add murder to that list of charges you're already facing." Jack leaned to the left to dodge a cobweb.

"Actually, if we see any insects or rodents in our pod, we contact Small Creature Control. We then vacate the pod until they safely remove the small creatures and find them another place to live."

"And what if they can't get rid of them?" Jack asked.

"It's never happened to me, but in that case, The Group moves the person to a new pod."

Jack snorted. "It gets loonier by the second."

In some spots water dripped from the tunnel top. Every now and then, tree roots poked through the top and sides.

"Sure is wet in here," Allen said.

"Yes, it is." Thomas stepped over a small puddle. "If you have to get through here in a hurry, you'll have to be careful not to fall."

A couple of garter snakes slithered in front of Jack. "Man, this place gives me the heebie-jeebies. What do you think, Pete?"

Peter followed right behind Thomas and walked hunched over. He repeatedly rubbed his hair. "Yeah, this is definitely a place you want to visit but not stay. I keep feeling like I have bugs and cobwebs in my hair."

"Hang in there, everyone." Thomas kept the light shining ahead. "It's about a hundred yards long, and we're almost to the end."

"We can't get there soon enough to suit me," Jack said. "It's so musty in here I probably already got a crop of mold growing in my beard."

"Here we go." Thomas shined his light on a set of rickety wooden steps. "Now, we just step up here."

"Now, wait," Peter said. "How do we know what's waiting for us out there? We could walk right into a whole bevy of thugs. You could have some waiting to greet us right now."

"I do wish you would trust us," Thomas said. "We've been out here all these years just like you. If we're going to make this work, you're going to have to let your guard down a bit."

Peter took one last swipe at the bugs and cobwebs he seemed to think were in his hair. "Nope, sorry. The guard stays up for a good long while. It's too dangerous out here for it not to be up."

"Sorry you feel that way," Thomas said, "but we want what's best for you. What's best for you is best for us and vice versa. It's all about the group."

Way stopped worrying about bugs and furrowed his brow. "What did you just say?"

Thomas's eyes widened, and he put his fingers to his chest. "Me? It was nothing, just pointing out that what's good for one of us is good for all of us." He took a step up.

"Come on. Let's see what's out there." Allen maneuvered around Peter and onto the first step." He turned back and grasped Peter's shoulder. "Lighten up on them. We could have a good deal here if we don't blow it."

Thomas pushed open the door, and sunlight rushed in. "That's right. You don't want to blow it." He nodded toward Allen. "Now, there's a young man who has some wisdom."

Everyone squinted hard, adjusting to the first rays of morning sunlight.

Thomas stepped out of the tunnel, followed by the others. "Here you go. Now if you have to use the tunnel, you know where you end up."

Oak and maple trees among others surrounded the opening. The forest side of the tunnel door was covered with vines. Bushes surrounded the opening to the point there wasn't much room for the men to spread out once they left the tunnel.

"See what a good spot this is." Thomas turned off his flashlight and put it in his pocket. "There are so many trees and so much underbrush, you ought to be able to get out of the tunnel and be safe from the Corpsmen. You have a good hiding place right here. I'd suggest if you have to come out here without Bart or me, that you wait inside the tunnel for a bit, listen for anything that sounds like it doesn't belong, and then ease out when it's clear. Once you're out, I'd say you hang loose here a little while. You should be well-covered until things settle down."

"Sounds like a plan," Allen said. "What do you think, Peter?"

Peter studied the surroundings. He cupped his hands above his eyes and looked back toward the cabin. "This might be all right. You can't even see the cabin from here."

"These are some mighty thick woods." Thomas rubbed his chin. "The Corpsmen would have a hard time finding you, us, anyone out here even if they did find that cabin."

Peter rubbed his neck. "What do you think, Jack?"

Jack mirrored Peter, then stroked his beard. "Well, Pete, this might do. Someone said we're about a hundred yards from the cabin here? That's closer than I ever want to be to them goons, but it's better than just being separated by the walls of that cabin."

"I like it," Allen said. "This works great. I think we'd be safe. It would at least give us a good head start if it comes time to run."

"It might," Peter said. "Of course, I'm afraid the thugs are like cockroaches, if you see one that means there's thousands you don't see. They could swarm from the cabin to here and all around. But this is probably about the best we can do."

"Glad it meets with your approval." Thomas took his flashlight out of his pocket. He smiled. "I guess as much as anything I offer will meet your approval anyway."

Peter smirked. "Got to protect my people." He peered into the tunnel. "By the way, there seems to be a lot of footprints in there. Fresh ones. Where did they all come from?"

Thomas rolled his eyes. "Here we go again. Well, friend, we did just have six men stomping through there. And as much as I like to think I'm graceful as a gazelle, we would more closely resemble the proverbial bull in a china closet. It wasn't six ballerinas walking in there, you know."

"Granted, we might be what you'd call kind of oafish," Peter said, "but still I believe if we took the trouble to match up shoe prints we'd find prints in there that we wouldn't find on our feet right now."

"Come on, man." Allen sighed. "What does he have to do?"

"That's all right." Thomas shined the light into the tunnel. "There are simple explanations. First, Bart and I have been in and out of this thing several times just making sure it's in good shape. We don't always wear the same shoes. If you'll notice back at the cabin, the Lord has blessed us each with more than one pair of shoes. And, it wasn't that long ago that we had more people."

"Yeah, well, what happened to those people?" Peter asked. "Where are they?"

Thomas turned off the flashlight. "There were fifteen of us. For several months we held steady at that. As time went on it was one thing and another. Some of them, a family of four, the dad got antsy like you and said they needed to move on. They weren't comfortable staying in one place all the time, thought the Corpsmen would find us. There were three more that just got too old, and it caught up with them. They were older than your lady, Mom, and not as healthy. There was nothing we could do for them and they passed. Then we had about six that went out hunting and scavenging and never came back. That was about four weeks ago, I'd say. I figure either the Corpsmen got them, or they wanted to move on but didn't have the backbone to tell us. So that left Bart and me. Isn't that right, Bart?"

Bart nodded. "Right."

Way studied Peter a few seconds. He looked back at Bart, who had a thick neck, barrel chest and biceps that looked to be about as big as Way's thighs.

Peter shifted his weight. "Where's the graves?"

"Huh?" Thomas seemed caught off guard. He leaned an ear closer to Peter. "Excuse me."

"Where's the graves?" Peter raised his eyebrows. "The graves. Where did you bury the folks that died? Where are they?"

"Uh, well, they're …," Thomas blustered a bit, before settling down. "We cremated them, scattered their ashes in the woods. It's not a pleasant thought, but we figured burying them would just attract animals or promote disease."

Peter scoffed. "Convenient."

Allen nodded. "Makes perfect sense. I can't see a problem with that."

Peter took several steps away from the tunnel opening. "Would you guys come here?" He motioned for Jack, Allen, and Way to join him. "Excuse us a minute, Thomas."

Jack, Allen, and Way joined Peter.

"What is it, Pete?" Jack asked.

"Yeah, what's wrong?" Allen said.

"We need to be careful." Peter pointed an index finger for emphasis.. "We don't know these guys. Some things aren't adding up. Jack, you've wandered these woods a long, long time, how long has it been since you saw someone out here you didn't know?"

Jack tucked his chin and raised his shoulders. "Oh, goodness, I don't know. The years have all run together, but it's been a good, long spell, I reckon."

"'A good, long spell,' huh?" Peter bent and leaned on his knees. "And, the man has a working flashlight. Jack, how long has it been since you've seen a working flashlight? Just think how old those batteries would be. He couldn't have brought them out of the city with him when things went bad. Where would that man have come up with a thirty-year-old battery that still had juice?"

"Don't you think he could have just come up with good, long-lasting batteries?" Allen asked. "I was only six when we came out here, but I know in our scavenging we've come across battery packages that say they're good for ten or fifteen years or whatever.

Isn't it possible his group came across some that lasted longer than expected?"

"Yeah, or maybe he brought fresh batteries out of the city with him and forgot to keep his flashlight hidden from us," Peter said.

"Why don't you ask him?"

Peter's frustration was obvious in his slumping shoulders and tilting head. "Really?" He touched a finger to his temple. "Think. If he brought that flashlight out of the city with him you think he's going to admit it?"

"Well, I don't know." Allen shrugged. "Maybe it would trip him up. I just think you're being too quick to judge."

Peter stepped toward Allen. A vein on the side of his forehead stood out. "We have to judge quick out here. If we trust the wrong people or make any wrong moves we could end up back in the city with those thugs torturing us and a crowd cheering while they do it. I don't think any of us want that."

Allen bowed his head. "Well, no, but I still think there is a better way than challenging him on every point or being contrary about everything,"

Peter rubbed his beard. "All right. Maybe I can tone down the doubts, at least out loud." He touched a finger to his head. "But they'll still be going on up here. I'm not about to give them the keys to the kingdom without knowing a lot more about them."

"Sorry to interrupt," Thomas said, "but are you fellows about ready to get back to the cabin? Bart's hungry. He's going to start chewing the bark off a tree if we don't get him back to the cabin."

Peter stared hard at Allen. "Don't go all in just yet. We need to learn more about these guys." He started back to the tunnel. "Yeah, we're coming," he said to Thomas.

CHAPTER 10—HUNTING

Before sunrise the next morning, Way, Peter, Jack, Thomas, and Bart went hunting while Mom, Allen, and Moses stayed at the cabin.

Leading the way, Peter stepped over a fallen tree. "Pay attention, Way. Jack's the best there is at setting traps. He can catch us a deer, rabbit, squirrel, you name it. He can even get us a bear so you can have a nice coat this winter."

Way followed Peter over the log and along the trail. "Yes, sir."

"Glad to hear Jack is so adept." Thomas brought up the rear. "Our best outdoorsman was in that last group I told you about. The one that went out and never came back."

Jack adjusted the pack slung over his shoulder. "Really? What was his name? Maybe I ran into him in the woods sometime."

"Hmm, his name was Marshall Gilmore." Thomas's voice carried in the morning air. "I doubt you would've had any encounters with him, though. He kept to himself, especially when out in the woods. If he saw or heard you, he probably would have made sure you didn't see or hear him."

Jack harumphed. "Don't sound very Christian. Most folks I met out here been more than happy to visit a spell, maybe pitch in with some help, give or take advice."

"I don't know about all that." Thomas waved his bow. "Marsh wasn't much of one for getting to know people."

"Glad I ain't like that," Jack said. "Getting to know people is how I met up with Pete and his bunch, and that's why I'm alive today." He stopped walking and hooked a thumb around an overall strap. "I just wish I'd been there to help my people when them thugs came to our settlement."

"Don't be hard on yourself," Peter said over his shoulder. "If you'd been there, those thugs would've got you, and you wouldn't be here to help us now. We wouldn't have had that great chicken dinner the other day, and I wouldn't be so confident we're going to have a successful hunt today."

"Thank you, boss man." Jack had both thumbs hitched around his overall straps. "That means a lot."

"You've been a big help to us all these years, brother, and it has been appreciated." Peter leaned left to avoid a low hanging elm branch. "Say, Thomas, what kind of hunting have a you all mostly done around here?"

Thomas took a couple of steps. "Oh, like you said earlier deer, rabbit, squirrel, you name it. The occasional bear for its coat and so on."

"Do you go out hunting specifically for grizzlies?" Peter asked.

"Well—"

Jack interrupted. "What do you mean, Pete? You know—"

Peter held a finger to his lips. "Shh, Jack. Let the man answer. I'm curious what kind of luck they've had finding grizzlies around here."

Thomas stopped. "Oh, I don't know. A fair amount, I guess. Like I said, Marshall took care of most of our hunting, and he would bring in the occasional grizzly bear."

"Are you sure they were grizzlies? Sometimes it's hard to tell the difference between a black bear and a grizzly." Peter shot a quick glance toward Jack.

"Oh, they were grizzlies, all right." Thomas gestured as he spoke. "I mean, Marshall was the expert, but he was very sure of himself and said they were grizzlies." He looked satisfied with his answer.

"Bart, you're being quiet. Is that what you picked up from this Marshall fellow?" Peter walked the trail and kept his eyes forward.

"Um, yes. Yes, he said they were grizzly bears.".

"So did you two do much of the hunting for your bunch?" Peter asked.

"Nah, I'm afraid to my shame, I wasn't involved in a lot of hunting," Thomas said. "Neither of us were. Now I wish I would have been more involved and learned as much as I could from Marshall. With his talents in the outdoors, I just never dreamed he would be one who got captured. I figured I'd be gone long before he was. Is that how it is with you, Bart?"

Bart grunted. "Yes, I'd say that describes me as well."

Peter stopped at a fork in the trail. He rubbed his chin. "We're going to split up here for a bit. Jack you come with Way and me, and we'll let Thomas and Bart stay together. I think they're probably better outdoorsmen than they're letting on. They're just being humble. That sound fair enough, Thomas?"

Thomas raised his shoulders. "Sounds fair enough. Bart?"

Bart mimicked Thomas's movement. "Fair enough."

"All right then." Peter pointed to the trail that went right. "You guys go that way. We'll take the one to the left. Let's meet back here in a couple of hours."

Jack adjusted his cap. "Say, Tom, you probably don't have to go a long way down the trail. These woods are pretty thick, and it ain't too hard to get hid good in them."

"Okay. Thank you," Thomas said as he and Bart started on the trail.

Peter watched the two of them disappear around a bend. He pulled Jack and Way close. "I don't know that those two can really do any good hunting on their own, but I didn't want any of us to be alone with either of them out here. I don't care what Allen says, I'm still not comfortable with them." He gripped Jack's shoulder. "You know as well as I do there's no grizzlies in this part of the country."

It was like the light turned on for Jack. "Oh, I see." He offered a big nod. "That's why you shushed me when I started to say that."

"Right." Peter smiled and patted Jack. "You got it. I think you might just make a decent help yet."

Jack returned the smile. "Yep. Once again, we see why you're the boss man."

Peter scoffed. "Hardly. Anyway, the flashlight with the good battery, the grizzly thing. There are other things that just don't add up."

Jack stroked his beard. "I see what you mean. I guess we do need to be careful."

"Way, you've been awful quiet," Peter said. "Do you have any thoughts on these fellows?"

"Uh, well," Way eyed the trail where Thomas and Bart had gone.

"Yeah," Jack said, "is there anything about them that might tell you if they're some of them what you call Corpsmen?"

"I … I don't know. I'm not used to things like that, I'm just used to seeing what's right in front of me. In the city, everything is clear. We didn't have to worry about if someone was who they said. We knew who the Corpsmen were, and we knew that everyone we talked to or dealt with was likely to turn us in if we went against anything The Group said."

Nodding, Jack clicked his tongue. "Comforting."

Peter rubbed his knife handle with a light touch. "Living out here all these years has taught us to be on the lookout. We've had to be careful around other folks, and we've had to fight and scrape for everything we've got. Don't get me wrong, the Lord has blessed us good, but part of that blessing is giving us the fortitude to carry on and fight."

Way took in a deep breath. "It was simpler in the city. The Group saw that we were taken care of, had food and shelter, a task. Everything we needed was right there."

"We've gone into it before." Peter continued to fidget with the knife handle. "That Group of yours gave you everything, but in return it expected everything you had."

Jack removed his cap and toyed with it. "I know you don't know business dealings the way me and Pete do, but it was basically a business deal." Jack held his cap about waist high and gently waved it. "Nowadays, back in your city and everywhere else, the business deal is they provide everything you need and you live your life serving them, doing what they say. You get it?"

"Well put," Peter said.

"I think I understand." Way knit his brow. "Why don't you two want to be part of that deal?"

Peter scratched his head and exhaled sharply. "Not to speak for Jack, but for me it starts and ends with Jesus. You said something to the effect that all religions are accepted by your Group, even Christianity. But you know and said this yourself, they only allow Christianity when the Christian is willing to accept other religions. But Jesus himself said he's the only way to get to God the Father, the only way to get to Heaven."

"The Group says all religions are the same. That they all go to this Heaven you're talking about."

Jack put his cap on. "Remember, your Group bunch also told us that Mom and your boy was captured. They lied to you, son. That's what they's all about."

Way held his fingers to his stomach. "All this talk makes my stomach feel funny."

"That's 'cause you're hearing the truth, and it goes against everything them devils been telling you your whole life." Jack pulled his cap down tight.

"But like I told you before, The Group takes care of me and gives me everything I need."

A squirrel in a nearby oak tree chattered and worked on an acorn.

Peter pressed Way's back. "Let's talk while we walk. I don't like having this conversation standing still when those two might show up." He took the lead as they started on the trail. "I get what you say about that Group giving you everything you need, but you need to see that they require everything you have. Before you escaped with your boy, when was the last time you made a decision for yourself?"

Way scratched his neck. "Oh, I don't know. Maybe it was when Luka and I decided to have him. The Group does allow us to choose whether or not to have offspring."

"And what are the consequences?" Peter stepped over a root that jutted out of the ground. "Even in a free world, choices have consequences. I'm sure that Group of yours can come up with some doozies."

"'Consequences'? 'Doozies'?" Way raised one side of his upper lip.

Peter sidestepped a low-hanging branch and held it out of the way for Way and Jack to pass. "Yeah, consequences, basically, it's what you have to deal with after you do something or make a decision. And, doozies," he chuckled, "well, that's just sort of a homey way of saying something's kind of wild or out there, outlandish. Understand?"

Way found himself at the head of the line. He stepped aside for Jack and Peter to pass. "I think so. The consequences for having an offspring? Hmm." He put his fingers to his chin. "Okay, for each offspring you have, every member of the unit gets fewer calories per day. Before partners have an offspring, they each get two thousand calories a day. After they have an offspring, their calories are cut to seventeen hundred and fifty. If they add another offspring to the unit, their calories are cut to fifteen hundred per day."

"Wow." Jack patted his protruding belly. "Don't believe I'd make it."

"Actually, sir …," Way paused and took a couple of deep breaths, "that's your number of calories if your overall weight is satisfactory. Outside of that, The Group determines how many calories you get per day based on if you need to gain or lose weight.

I'm afraid with your girth, The Group would cut you to a thousand or twelve hundred calories per day until your weight reached a satisfactory level."

"You mean until they starved me to death!" Jack palmed his belly. "You're killing me, man."

"You see, Way, that's just it." Peter had his spot at the front of the line again. "Yes, I'm all for eating healthy and taking care of yourself, but the government shouldn't be in the business of telling a man what he can and can't eat. Then to cut your calories because you have kids, it boggles my mind."

"'Kids'? 'Boggles'?" Way was lost. "I've heard you say kid before, but not boggles."

"Oh, boy." Peter scratched his head. "Kids, that's what we call children. Your boy, Moses, he's a kid. It's pretty informal. Boggles. Well, that's something confounding or confusing. Something like that."

"I get it," Way said. "Anyway, The Group cuts calories when you have these kids, as you call them, so you think it through before you use up earth's resources. Every kid uses up that much more and takes away from what everyone else can have. And as far as cutting calories for the overweight, The Group wants everyone to be healthy and not be a drain on society. It's very similar to the issue with these kids. If one person eats more than their share, it takes away from the earth's resources."

Peter scuffed along the trail, kicking up dust. "You were willing to give up some of your calories to have your boy?"

"Yes." Way nodded although he was at the back of the line and neither Peter nor Jack could see him. "There was just something in me that made me think it was worth it."

"What did your woman think of that?" Jack asked.

"She wasn't as committed as I was. But she was willing to give it a try for the first year and see how she felt then. Turns out that was enough for her."

"Did she miss her calories too much?" Jack lumbered around a bush that encroached on the trail.

Following Jack, who had Shamus at his heels, Way maneuvered around the same bush. "It wasn't so much the calories. She's not much of an eater anyway. It was mostly the inconvenience. She thought the boy, Moses, kept her from advancing at her task, and we had to take care of him almost twelve hours a day. She said those three hours an evening between when we picked him up from the Education Center and put him to bed at night were torture for her. Just too much for her, took away too much of her freedom."

Peter huffed. "Like there was freedom to take away."

"Amen," Jack said.

Peter came to an area that was especially thick with bushes surrounding a tree. "This look all right to you, Jack?"

"Whew." Jack stood straight and took off his cap. He whisked sweat from his forehead and studied the area. "Looks good. There's probably plenty of game that comes along here. Even if we don't see anything now, I got the stuff so I can set a few traps. We could come back later and check them."

"Sounds good," Peter said.

"So what do we do?" Way asked.

"Well, we got to be quiet. You're mostly going to watch and learn." Jack slipped his pack off his back and ducked into the bushes.

Peter joined Jack in the bushes. He motioned to Way. "Come on in."

The three men settled in, Shamus sat by Jack and the wait began. Way didn't have any problem keeping quiet. He didn't know what to do and didn't know what to say.

Occasionally Jack whispered instructions and pointed out things in the forest: squirrels chasing each other around a tree, a rabbit nibbling on blades of grass, sparrows flitting from branch to branch. Nothing came close enough for Peter or Jack to bother with loading their bows.

Several times Jack poked Way out of the state between awake and asleep.

About thirty minutes passed, and no deer wandered by. Peter and Jack continued to wait patiently. Way continued to battle sleep.

"Help!" came a cry from another part of the woods.

Peter and Jack sprang up.

"It's Thomas!" Peter said. He was out of the bushes and running toward the voice before Way even stood.

Jack was on Peter's heels. Shamus raced ahead.

"Wait!" Way bumbled through gathering his pack and getting out of the bush. By the time he got to the trail, Peter and Jack were out of sight, but he could hear them running and could also hear Thomas's cries.

Thomas and Bart were a couple of minutes away. When Way reached them, he saw Bart backing away from a black bear.

Thomas stood several feet away, his knife still in its sheath, his bow still looped around his torso and arrows still in their quiver. "Get away, Bart! Run!"

The bear, standing just a little taller than Bart, took a swipe at him and hit him across the face.

Bart screamed.

"Run!" Thomas yelled.

"No!" Peter yelled. He was standing beside Jack. "He'll chase you!"

Bart continued to back away.

The bear growled and swung again.

Shoulders drawn in and head ducked, Bart shielded his face and torso with his fists and forearms.

The bear took a swipe at Bart's side. It ripped his shirt and drew blood.

From thirty feet away and behind the bear, Jack loaded his bow and took aim.

"No!" Thomas yelled. "Don't shoot it! That's not right!"

Shamus barked. He danced at Jack's feet.

Bart backed against a tree and continued to shield himself.

"Steady, fellow." Jack continued to hold the bowstring back with his forefinger touching the corner of his mouth.

The bear raised its paw, ready to strike again.

Jack released the string, the arrow flew true and hit the bear in the back, between the shoulders.

The bear yowled and writhed. It turned toward Jack and Peter and charged.

Growling, Shamus ran for the bear.

Peter loaded his bow and shot the onrushing bear in the chest.

Another yowl. The bear took two steps. It staggered from one side to the other and fell face first. It took a gurgled breath. Then another. It was silent.

Way's heart pounded.

Bart fell to his knees, holding his side. Thomas went to him.

Peter swiped a wrist across his forehead. He glared at Thomas. "Were you just going to stand there and let that thing kill him?"

Kneeling beside Bart, Thomas examined his side. "I didn't know what to do. I froze."

"You've been out here almost thirty years and still don't know how to act in an emergency?" Peter ran his fingers through his hair. "That thing was going to kill him, and you just stood there telling us not to shoot it." He went to Bart.

Thomas didn't make eye contact with Peter, but checked Bart's gashed side. "It's one of God's creatures. We can't kill God's creatures."

Peter's mouth fell open, and he dropped his bow. "'Can't kill God's creatures'? What is wrong with you? That 'God's creature' was getting ready to maul your friend. Mister, I don't know how you've made it out here all these years, but that's crazy. On top of that, we were hunting. I was hunting animals for food. What did you plan to shoot with that bow and arrow? Daisies? It's times like this that I wish I cussed 'cause I'd really like to tell you what I think."

"We …, we were in its territory," Thomas said. "It was defending its territory."

"I don't know what kind of bunch you all were part of," Peter shook his head, "but human life comes before animal life. I don't care where you are or whose territory it is, human life comes first."

Thomas continued to focus on Bart's side. "The Group wouldn't approve."

Peter's eyes widened. "Come again."

"Uh, what I meant was that we're already in trouble with The Group, and killing that creature would just make things worse."

"Buddy, if you're a believer and you've lived in the woods thirty years and done anything near like we have, you're in deep enough trouble with that bunch that killing one bear isn't going to make any difference." Peter motioned for Way to join him. "What do you think, Way? That Group bunch raised you, but you've been out here with us a while now. What do you think of us killing that bear to save Bart?"

Way rubbed his forehead. "When I first came out here, I'm afraid I would have chosen to let it live, but little by little, I see your point. I think you were right to kill it."

Jack stood over the bear, checking it out. "Fellows there ain't nothing to argue about now. We got us a bear. We may not want to eat it, they's kind of greasy, and the meat don't taste much good, but we can sure put this thing to use somehow."

"But what if some Corpsmen were to capture us and find us with that thing in our possession?" Thomas asked.

"Like Pete said," Jack knelt by the bear, "we're in so deep now that ain't going to make much difference." He groaned as he stood. "My old bones are about wore out. Way, let's you and me gather some sticks and branches and rig up a kind of a sled to pull this bear on." He pointed to Bart. "I reckon we also need one for him, too."

A couple of hours later, Mom stepped out of the cabin, onto the porch to greet the hunters. "What happened to you all?"

Allen followed her out, holding Moses. "What's going on?"

Peter motioned toward Bart, who was lying on the sled. "Our friend here had a run-in with a bear, and even though the bear got the worst end of it, he didn't come out of it in any too good of shape."

"Let me take a look." Mom stepped off the porch. She bent over Bart's side, examining the wound. "Oh my, he got you good." She stood straight. "Get him inside, and lay him on the couch. Brother Peter, would you get me some good, clean water? And, Brother Jack, I need a hot compress. Would you get that going for me?"

"Yes, ma'am." Jack went to work.

Thomas helped Bart to the couch. Mom moved Bart's tattered shirt out of the way and checked the gash.

Bart winced when Mom hit a tender spot.

"Oh, I'm sorry." Mom drew back.

Bart took a deep breath. "That's all right." He craned his neck and found Peter and Jack in the kitchen taking care of the tasks Mom had given them. "By the way, thank you for what you did out there."

"You're welcome." Peter poured water into a large bowl.

"Ditto." Jack put a log on the fire in the wood stove.

Chapter 11—Discovery

A couple of hours later, Peter, who had been outside helping Jack skin the bear, came inside. Way followed.

"How's he doing, Mom?" Peter asked.

Mom sat in the chair beside Bart, who was asleep on the couch. "I got that gash cleaned about as good as I could, and I've changed his compress several times, trying to keep a hot one on it. He might end up with some infection, but I believe with a little doctoring and a lot of praying, he'll be all right."

Peter rubbed his bearded cheeks. "I figure we can't leave here for a couple of days if we wanted to, right?"

"You're right, brother." Mom clasped Bart's shoulder. "I don't like sitting still any more than you do, but I got to at least see Brother Bart up and moving before I can go anywhere."

Peter pursed his lips. "I figured."

"Mom?" Way stood behind Peter.

"Yes, son?"

"If you would like to take a bit of a break, I can watch him. I don't know that I can take care of any medical attention, but as long as he's sleeping and doesn't need anything, I should be all right."

Mom stood and pressed the wrinkles out of her too-big jeans. "Why, thank you." She went to Way and gripped his forearm. "That's very considerate of you. I could use a little break." She turned to Peter. "Brother Peter, why don't we go outside and you show me what you all are doing with that bear?"

Way watched them leave the cabin. He went to the chair beside Bart and sat. Outside, Moses squealed as Allen chased him. Shamus joined them, barking his excitement over the game. The bed in one of the other rooms squeaked. Way didn't know if Thomas was asleep or awake, but he was moving. The bed squeaked again.

Way picked at a loose thread on the chair. Bart's breathing was slow and deep. Way studied him.

Another squeak from the other room.

Bart wriggled and moved from lying on his back to lying on his left side, facing the room. Holding his fingers at his chin, he wrapped his right hand over his left.

Something caught Way's attention, and he leaned closer to Bart.

The bed squeaked again.

Way squinted.

The bed squeaked.

Outside, Moses squealed.

There it was. Way leaned closer, studying the slightest bump on back of Bart's right hand. Way's pulse quickened.

Way shifted his attention to the spot where The Group implanted the chip on his first birthday. The chip he ripped out the night he escaped the city.

Way reached toward Bart.

The bed squeaked.

Way sat upright and pulled back.

He watched the hallway opening. No one came.

Again, Way leaned closer and stretched his shaking hand toward Bart's. With a slight touch, he felt the bump. It rolled back and forth under his finger.

The bed in the other room squeaked.

Way pulled back. He looked around the room. He looked outside where Allen growled and Moses squealed.

Way stood. He took a deep breath.

Squeak. Squeak. Squeak. Squeak. Approaching steps.

Thomas appeared in the hall entryway. He smiled. "What's wrong? You look scared."

Way's heart pounded. "No. I, uh, I …," As hard as he thought, no words came.

Thomas moved closer. "Is something wrong? You seem more frightened than Bart was when the bear attacked him."

"No. It's …, I …," Way rubbed his palms together.

Thomas put an arm around Way's shoulder. He seemed to increase his three-inch height advantage. "Are you sure there's nothing wrong? Can I help?"

"No." Way's face grew hot, but he also felt that all the blood had left his head. He swayed. He blinked hard and took a deep breath. "No. Thank you." Words finally came. "I'm all right. I was just …, I thought he seemed to be having trouble and that maybe I needed to get Mom."

Thomas patted Way's back. "That's good of you, but if he has trouble, I'd rather you get me than one of them. He and I have known each other quite some time, and I'm probably better equipped to help him than Mom or any of your other friends."

Way wanted to see Thomas's hand, see if there was a bump on it, see how it felt. He nodded. "All right. I'll remember that. I was just concerned."

"That's good of you." Thomas continued to pat Way's back. "I appreciate that, and I appreciate Mom's medical attention, neanderthal as it is, but, please, if there are any concerns from this point on, come to me."

Way bowed his head. "Yes, sir."

"Good fellow." Thomas gave Way one last pat. "Good fellow."

I have to tell Peter. God, please get me out of here. Way caught himself. *I think I prayed to a God I don't even believe in.*

Thomas apparently caught a strange look on Way's face. "Are you sure nothing is wrong?"

"I'm sure." Way gave a slight head shake. "I'm fine. Just thinking of some things I need to do to help around here."

Outside, Allen growled. Moses squealed. Shamus barked.

Way saw his opportunity. He stepped toward the door. "I better get out here and help with my son. I don't want to completely turn him over to someone else to watch and entertain."

"Yes. Yes. Do that," Thomas said. He paused, apparently mulling something over. "I take it you and the boy haven't been out here long."

Way tried to think of an answer, but it seemed the only thing that would work was the truth. It wouldn't be hard for Thomas to find out from one of the others that Moses and he had recently escaped the city. And if Peter's apparent suspicions and the bump on Bart's hand were any indication, Thomas probably knew the whole story.

"Right." Way couldn't look Thomas in the eye. "It was the night before his mother was to say whether he would continue or be extinguished. She planned to have him extinguished, and I couldn't bring myself to let that happen, so I escaped with him. Peter and another man found us in the woods and took us in."

"Has there been loss of life since you joined these people?"

Way lowered his head. "Yes."

"Then did you really escape?"

Bart rolled on his back and groaned.

Way was thankful for the momentary diversion, but couldn't put off answering the question too long. "I don't know. I guess not. We're still running, and we're still limited in what we can do."

Thomas pressed his fingertips together at his waist. He tilted his head a bit to one side. "Have you considered turning yourself in?"

Peter threw open the door. "No, he hasn't!" His face was red and his eyes full of fire. "What are you doing? Why are you trying to talk him into turning himself in?"

Thomas took a step back. "No. I just asked if he had considered it. I know it would be death for him and the boy, but it would save the rest of us. Sometimes you have to consider what's best for the group."

"Best for the group, huh?" Peter stood beside Way. "You know, you sound like you could've come straight from that bunch."

"No, no, no." Thomas seemed to make a point of speaking slow and calm. "It's just that sometimes an individual has to make a sacrifice for the good of others."

Peter squared his shoulders. "No one here is going to turn themselves in, especially not him. He's the one we're protecting. Him and his boy."

"Maybe, maybe he's right," Way said. "There's been nothing but trouble since I came along. You and the others have been good to Moses and me, but maybe I should turn myself in. Maybe then they would leave you and the others alone."

"No, you can't." Peter's demeanor shifted as he spoke to Way. "One, you got out of that place to protect Moses, so I'm sure you wouldn't want to take him back in there with you. That brings me to the second point. Moses needs you. A boy needs his dad. That boy needs you more than just about anything in the world. He needs you even more than the rest of our little family needs you."

"Family?" Way drew back his head.

"Yes, family." Peter pressed Way's back. "Me, Mom, Jack, Allen. We're family. We aren't blood related in the natural, but we're family. There's a bond between us. All the ones we've lost over the years have been family, too. Now, you and Moses are part of the family."

Way clicked his tongue. "Thank you. That means a lot."

"You're quite welcome." Peter eased Way toward the door. "Now let's get outside and see how Jack's doing with that bear."

The two of them went out leaving Thomas with Bart.

As soon as Way stepped off the porch, Moses saw him. "Dada!" Moses said and scurried toward Way on all fours.

Way picked up Moses, held him overhead and gave him a small, playful shake. He lowered Moses and held him close.

"See?" Peter said. "That boy needs you."

"Maybe so." Way gazed at Moses for a few seconds. He came out of it and leaned closer to Peter. "If we could, there's something I'd like to talk to you about." He looked around. Mom and Jack were getting anything useful they could from the bear carcass, Allen was sitting on the ground, legs crossed, where he had been playing with Moses. "Alone, if we could," Way whispered.

"Sure. Sure," Peter said. "Say, everyone, if you all will excuse us, Way and I are going to take Moses for a little walk in the woods."

With Way carrying Moses, he and Peter ambled along the trail away from the cabin. Way looked back over his shoulder and spotted Thomas watching out the window.

A few minutes later and a couple of hundred feet from the cabin, Way set Moses on the ground. Moses laughed and slapped the dirt raising a small dust cloud.

Way sat on a fallen tree. "I saw something I think I need to share with you."

"Yeah, go on." Peter furrowed his brow.

Way put a finger on the scar where his computer chip had been. "You know the chip I took out of my hand? The one that would have allowed The Group to track me?"

"Yeah."

Moses tried to put his finger on an ant.

"Well," Way continued, "I believe Bart has one."

Peter's eyes widened, and he tilted his head to one side. "Really? Great."

"Yes. When I was watching him, he turned and moved his hand. I noticed a small bump. I felt it, and it felt like a chip."

In trying to play with the ant, Moses squished it.

Peter massaged his forehead and took a deep breath. "That pretty well confirms my fears." He looked back toward the cabin.

"What can you do?"

Closing his eyes, Peter leaned his head forward and covered his eyes. "We have to get away from them. That Group bunch of yours must have sent them into the woods to get us. With those chips, the government thugs could find them and us anytime. They could show up any minute."

"What are you going to do?"

"I'll think of something. I just know we have to get away from them fast. We need to get back to the cabin. When we get there, just act natural. Don't let on that you know anything."

A few minutes later, Way, Peter and Moses made it back to the cabin. Moses rode on Way's shoulders. Mom, Jack, and Allen all worked with the bear carcass.

Thomas was with them, although Way thought it looked like the bloody process could make him sick anytime.

"You fellows have a nice walk?" Thomas asked.

"Pretty good." Peter answered without looking in Thomas's direction.

"You solve any problems?"

"Not a lot of problems to solve." Peter still watched the others work with the carcass. "Good as we have it right now, we don't have a lot to deal with."

Thomas chuckled. "That's good. Good that you have that outlook even though there is an enemy after us that has all the resources in the world at its disposal."

"Yeah," Peter shifted his weight, but kept his eyes on the carcass, "I know that whatever happens I'm, we're, on the winning side. That's quite comforting."

Thomas pursed his lips. "That it is. That it is."

Jack furrowed his brow. He glanced from Peter to Thomas and back to Peter. Way thought Jack wanted to say something but held back.

Way held Moses's feet to help him stay steady. Everyone was quiet. Allen fidgeted with his ear lobe. Mom was unusually focused on the dead bear.

The need for noise got the best of Way. "How is Bart doing?"

"Doing well," Thomas said. "He should be up and around in the next day or so."

"Good." Way nodded. "Good."

Peter rocked from heel to toe. "When Mom gets him fixed up, I believe we need to move on and let these fellows have their cabin back."

Allen's jaw dropped. "What? Why?"

"There's a few things." Peter continued his easy rock. "One, I believe we've imposed on them long enough. I'm sure they have their own fish to fry. And two, I believe the state has intensified its hunt for believers and others who just don't want to go along with its dictatorship. I believe the bigger a bunch we have and the longer we stay in one place, the easier it is for them to find us."

Thomas held his elbows at his side and had his palms up. "I know we've had our differences and run into some tension, but I believe it's best for all of us to stay together. There are things you people bring to the group. And there are things Bart and I bring to the group."

"I think he's right," Allen said. "I believe it's good for us to stay right here. This gives us a base, stability. I guess you could say a place to call home."

Peter stopped rocking. "Stability for people like us went out the window when that bunch took over. The only stability now is if you do what they say, when they say, how they say." He made a circle in the air taking in himself, Mom, Jack, Allen, Way, and Moses. "We need to talk it over among ourselves. There may be some things some of us don't feel free saying in front of Thomas."

"I have no problem with that," Thomas said. "I think Bart and I have made it clear how we can help the group. Showing you our tunnel was a show of great trust."

"Look," Allen said, "they brought us to their cabin, showed us their tunnel, contributed food. What more do you want from them?"

Way watched close, wondering if Peter would mention Bart's chip.

Peter bit his lower lip. He waved. "It's tough. We've been out here almost thirty years. It's hard to trust people. That Group bunch has tightened the screws the last few weeks. They won't be satisfied until they've wiped out everyone who doesn't want to be part of their party. So, yeah, it's hard for me to go gaga when new people show up out of the blue."

"What more can we do?" Thomas stepped toward Peter.

Peter ran his fingers through his hair. "Give me time. That's it. Give me time."

"You can have all the time you need." Thomas clicked his tongue. "We're all in this together. Stay here or leave, I think we should stick together."

"That doesn't surprise me." Peter nodded. "You seem, you seem like a teamwork kind of guy."

Thomas's face brightened in a great smile. "That I am, my friend. That I am. It's all about the group."

Peter took in a breath and held up a finger like he was about to speak, but paused. He lowered his finger. "Yeah, it's all about the group."

Chapter 12—Witness

A few hours later, Way and Peter sat in the front room. Way held the sleeping Moses in his lap. Bart slept on the couch. Mom, Jack, Allen, and Thomas were outside. Mom and Jack taught Allen and Thomas the finer points of parceling out the carcass, what could be used and what could be discarded.

"I've used the liver and heart from other animals as bait for fishing," Way heard Jack say. "I imagine a bear's organs would work just as well as a chicken's to catch catfish."

Way studied Peter. "I have a question."

Peter had his right ankle crossed over his left knee. "Fire away."

"What?"

Peter chuckled. "Ask your question."

"This Jesus and being a Christian, you seem to believe it a lot different than the Christians in the city."

"I do."

"Why? It's the same Jesus, the same religion."

Peter uncrossed his legs, leaned forward and rested his elbows on his knees. "It's different. Totally different. In your city, those who say they're Christians and believe in Jesus, they're watering it down."

"What?"

"They make it so it fits what they want, make it so it doesn't make them or anyone else uncomfortable. In the Bible, which I know you haven't read, and even if you had it would be some make-everyone-happy version, Jesus says he is the only way to the Father. There's no other way. Those people that you talk about in the city, they say Jesus is not the only way to the Father or he's not the only way to Heaven."

"Who's this Father?"

Peter leaned back and looked to the ceiling. "Lord, this is supposed to be so simple a child can understand it, please help me get it across to him."

Way lifted his gaze to the area of the ceiling where Peter looked.

Peter leaned forward again and rested his elbows on his knees. "God loves you. His son, Jesus, loves you. They love everyone. Even that grand poobah or whatever she is."

"Grand Matron."

Peter gave a dismissive wave. "Whatever. God loves you so much that he wants you to be with him in Heaven forever, all eternity, no end of time. He loves you so much that he wants to give you peace through all this with that Group bunch after us and those Corpsmen traipsing around trying to catch us." He tapped Way on the temple. "He wants you to be free from all the wrongheaded stuff that's been poured into your head your whole life."

Way felt sweat beads roll down his forehead. His stomach churned. He tugged at his shirt collar.

"It's nothing to be scared of." Peter patted Way's knee. "God loving you, wanting you to be with him forever and wanting to give you peace now is all good news. That's the gospel. Gospel means good news."

Way wrinkled his brow. "What's the bad news."

Peter sat back and exhaled. "That's a rough one. The bad news is eternity separated from God, eternal punishment, worse than anything that Group bunch could ever do to you. A place hotter than you can imagine. But I like to focus more on the good news and God's love. If you take care of the good news, you don't have to worry about the bad news."

"What is this gospel? This good news?"

Peter stood, smiling. He stretched. "It's been a long time since I shared the plan of salvation with someone, so I might be a little rusty. Let me get the Bible from my pack."

He disappeared down the hallway and came back with the tattered book they had shown Way earlier. He sat and opened the book. The cover was torn in several places and the pages were frayed. A couple of pages fell out.

"You do much reading?" Peter held the book toward Way.

Way wrinkled his nose and leaned back. "The Group provides us with the things it wants us to read. It's unlawful to read anything else."

Peter held up the Bible. "Reading is a way to communicate, a way to learn, get ideas across."

"We don't have to worry with that in the city. The Group tells us everything we need to know."

Peter lowered his head and rubbed his forehead. "Oh, boy. This is worse than I thought. No wonder they're able to control you people." He raised the Bible and gave it a slight shake. "This book tells you the most important thing you need to know. This right here tells you how great God is and how much he loves you."

"How come The Group never told me about this?"

"They're scared of him. They want to do their own thing, follow their own desires, not worry about what he says is right and wrong. They have their own ideas on that, and they have no interest in hearing or telling God's ideas on the matter. And they want to control people like you. If you can't get information for yourself and you can only get what they want you to get, they got you."

Bart stirred on the couch.

Peter looked to Bart, then back to the Bible. "I better tell you what I was going to tell you in the first place. If he wakes up, or Thomas comes in, it'll cramp our chances.

"First off, God exists and loves you, no matter what that Group bunch tells you. He wants you to be with him forever in Heaven. The first way that can happen is if you're perfect, if you never sin."

Way laid the sleeping Moses on the floor. After sitting back down, he leaned in and rested his elbows on his knees. "What's sin?"

"It's missing the mark, falling short of God's perfection. We're all born into it. Even Mom as good as she is and has been her whole life, as far as I can tell, was born into it." Peter motioned toward Moses. "Your boy there, cute as he is, those times you tell him not to do something, and he does it anyway, that's the born sinner in him. Back in the city, if you looked at a woman other than your wife with impure thoughts, that's sin. You take something from your task, something that doesn't belong to you, that's sin. You don't have to learn it, it's just in you. Before everything went bad, my preacher would explain it by saying you don't have to teach a child to steal from a cookie jar. Again, your boy, one of these days, you'll probably run into a situation where you know he did something, but to try to stay out of trouble he'll tell you he didn't do it. He won't have to learn that. It's born in him, born in all of us."

Way sat straight, eyes wide and sucked in a sharp breath through gritted teeth. "Sounds like everything is sin."

Peter chuckled. "Yeah, well, I guess sometimes it does." He raised his index finger. "But that's where the good news comes in. It's the second, but best, way to get to Heaven. God the Father knew none of us could live that perfect, sinless life, so he sent his Son, Jesus, to do it for us."

Way furrowed his brow. "I don't understand."

"Let me think." Peter put his fingers to his chin. "Think about when you escaped from the city with Moses. You did that because you love him so much. You're his dad, his father, and you love him. As much as you love Moses, God loves you more." He paused a second. "Infinitely more."

"Hmm." Way pursed his lips. He nodded. "Wow."

"Yeah. By God's laws and standards, sins cannot be forgiven without the shedding of blood. And that blood has to be sinless. Well, so you and I could be forgiven of our sins, Jesus came and lived that perfect life. He never took that cookie from the cookie jar, never lied to get out of trouble." He curled his lip. "None of it."

"For me?" Way put his fingers to his chest.

"Yes, for you and for me and for everyone. Not everyone accepts it, but that's what he did. You remember when we were in the woods and those drones flew in and were shooting at us?"

Way nodded.

Bart turned from one side to the other and faced the back of the couch.

Moses squirmed on the floor beside Way.

"Okay," Peter said, "when Abe covered you, so you wouldn't get hit, and he ended up getting hit and dying, he gave his life so you could live."

Way lowered his head.

"That's what Jesus did for us. We couldn't live that perfect life, so he came to earth and did it for us. Now all we have to do is accept, receive, what he did for us and we're good. What do you think?"

Way sat back, exhaling. "I don't know. This is all new."

"I'm sure it is." Peter leaned closer. "Keep it simple, though." He touched a finger to his temple. "Think about it. God loves you more than you love Moses, and Jesus sacrificed his life for you just the way Abe did."

"I don't know. It's different."

"Yes, it is. But think about it. Think about it hard. Jesus wants you free, and that Group bunch wants you under its thumb. You just have to believe he's God's Son, that he died for you and that he will forgive you of your sins if you ask. Crazy as it sounds, when you do that, he'll take a place in your heart." Peter gave Way a light touch to the chest.

With hesitation, Way lowered his head to see Peter's finger on his chest. He looked back up at Peter. "I'll think about it hard."

"You might want to make that hard *and* fast because I don't know how long we have. With these two in the mix and us not knowing exactly what that Group bunch has in mind for how to capture us, we don't know how long we have." Peter pointed toward the ceiling. "Accept Jesus like I said and it's forever in a place greater than we can ever imagine." He pointed to the floor. "Don't accept him and it's forever in a place of torment worse than we can ever imagine."

Way's chest rose with a deep breath. "I'll keep that in mind."

After dark that night, the whole group sat in the front room. Bart was able to sit on the couch, where he was joined by Jack and Allen. Mom and Thomas each had a chair. Peter and Way sat on the wooden floor. Moses sat on Way's lap, busying himself with a chunk of wood.

Peter stood and worked the kinks out of his legs. "Say, Thomas, do you mind excusing my friends and me? There are some things we need to talk about."

Thomas started to stand.

Peter gestured for Thomas to stop. "Oh, no, don't get up." He jerked his head toward the door. "We can go outside."

"Don't you think it would be good for all of us to be in on the talk?" Thomas asked. "Everything each of us does impacts the group. The group comes first."

Way stopped in the middle of getting up. *"The Group comes first."* That was one of the phrases Grand Matron Tannon used on the nightly recording played for all loyal world citizens. His blood ran cold. He got goosebumps. He looked at Thomas, then Peter.

Peter rubbed his face. He tugged at his ear lobe. "If it's all the same, first I'd like to meet with my folks. We'll be freer to say what we think if it's just us."

Thomas scoffed. "I haven't seen that you have a lot of trouble saying what you think."

Peter smiled and offered a quick nod and wink. "Thanks. I'll take that as a compliment."

"Don't you think we should let them in on the talk, too?" Allen said. "What one of us does affects all of us."

Peter started to the door. The heels of his boots scraped the floor. "Like I said, we'll be freer to say what we think if it's just us. We'll let them know anything that concerns them."

Allen grunted and stood. "Sorry, Thomas."

Peter, Jack, Allen, Mom, and Way, holding Moses, gathered at an oak tree about fifty feet from the cabin.

Jack tugged at the bill of his cap and shifted his weight. "What is it, boss man?"

Peter stepped to the middle of the circle formed by the others. He eyed the cabin. "Don't anyone panic, but I believe these guys are plants."

"Plants?" Allen said.

Mom leaned closer to Peter. "You mean you think the government put them here?"

Peter pursed his lips. "Yes, I do."

Jack removed his cap and scratched his head. "Oh, that's a peck of trouble. What do you think we should do?"

"Wait." Allen took turns looking from one friend to the other. "What makes you think they're from the government?"

Peter scratched his head. "There are several things. One, somehow they have a flashlight with a good battery. Two, they didn't know we don't have grizzly bears around here. Three, when that bear attacked Bart, Thomas wouldn't kill it, not even to save his so-called friend. Another thing, when they first came along, Thomas said, 'Jesus is Lord of lords and King of kings.' We all know, well, all of us but Way, know that's backwards from the way we say it to identify believers."

Allen closed his eyes tight and grimaced. He leaned his head forward. He raised his head. "I know that's backwards from how the Bible usually uses it, and I know the way it's in the Bible is the way we've greeted people over the years to test them, but it could just be that he made a mistake, got it backwards by accident."

"Or, was told the wrong way by someone they captured," Peter said, "so when a situation like this came along believers like us would have a clue that these guys aren't what they say they are?"

"You don't have any proof," Allen said. "You're taking coincidences and making these men guilty. They were good enough to bring us to their cabin. They showed us a secret tunnel."

Peter ran his fingers through his hair. "And I can just about guarantee you if we're ever in a pinch and think we need to use that thing, we're going to open up that door out in the woods and be met by more government thugs than you can shake a stick at." He nodded toward Way. "Tell them what you told me."

Way rubbed his palms together. "I'm sure as I can be that Bart has a chip in the back of his hand, a chip like I had, a chip like all world citizens have."

Mom gasped.

Jack pulled his hat down tight. "Oh, that ain't good, Pete. That ain't good at all."

Way took a deep breath and continued. "Also, Thomas uses phrases that were part of what we world citizens heard played through the night every night, like 'The Group comes first,' and others."

"Well, the group does come first." Allen waved. "We have to take care of each other, watch out for each other."

"This group." Peter made a circular motion. "We have to worry about this group, take care of this group." He poked a thumb toward the cabin. "I think stuff like that is so deeply ingrained in him that he says it without even thinking."

Allen's eyes were wide and wild. "Mom? Jack? What about this? What do you honestly think?" He snapped his fingers. "We can't pronounce these men guilty just like that. This is crazy."

Jack hung his head. "I don't know, son."

An owl hooted in the distance.

Mom took off her glasses and wiped the lenses. "What you say is true. We don't have proof. But on the other side of the coin, Brother Peter is a good man and a good leader. With the Lord's help, he's brought us through a lot of hard times."

Jack hitched a thumb around the strap of his overalls. "I'd have to agree with Mom. Maybe we don't have proof, but the old boss man's taken good care of us. He does his level best to see that we're all safe and secure. If he thinks them fellows are plants, I'd be inclined to go along with him."

Allen scratched his head. "I think he's a good leader, too, a great one even. But I think he's missing the mark on this, going down the wrong path."

"What would you propose we do?" Peter asked.

"Talk to them." Allen broke the formation and paced. "Get more information. Find out for sure if they are from the state."

Peter cocked his head to one side. "You do know if they're from that Group bunch and they do have chips implanted, that we could have droves of thugs on us any second without warning."

Allen stopped pacing.

"We don't have time to get information," Peter continued, "or find out who sent them and why they showed up all of a sudden. We have to treat this like we have seconds to deal with it, not weeks or months. We have to consider that their back-up or whatever could drop out of the sky any second."

"Or that some of them flying machine guns could show up anytime." Jack pointed to the sky.

Moses wiggled, wanting down.

Way tightened his hold on Moses. "Hold on, boss man."

Peter turned to Way. "Yes?"

"Oh." Way blinked. "I'm sorry. I was talking to Moses."

Peter gave a firm nod. "I'll take it as a compliment that you used one of Jack's names for me for your boy."

Jack toyed with the bill of his cap. "And I'll take it as a compliment that you thought highly enough of one of my names for Pete to use it for your boy."

"I'm glad to see we're all in such complimentary moods." Allen paced again. "But what do you propose, Peter? If you're so sure Thomas and Bart are from the government, what do we do?"

Peter stroked his beard. "We have to get away from them. Plain and simple."

The cabin door opened. A figure stepped on to the porch. "Are you all right?" It was Thomas.

"We're fine," Peter said. "Just deciding what we need to do."

"I was just checking, wanted to make sure no bears had attacked you." Thomas laughed and went back inside.

A coyote howled. Another answered. And then another.

"I guess we better wrap this up." Peter started toward the cabin. "We have to get away from them soon. Just remember, be careful what you say or do around them, where you go with them. Everything. Watch out. Expect it to go bad."

Chapter 13—Judgment

A few hours later, Way woke up when Peter burst into the room where he and Allen slept.

"We have to go!" Peter yelled. "We have to get out of here! Get as much as you can as fast as you can, and let's go!"

The room was dark.

"What? Why?" Allen said.

"Come on! Let's just go!" Peter shined a flashlight in the room.

Allen held up a forearm, shielding his eyes from the light. "What's going on?"

Peter hurried to Allen's side and pulled the blanket off him. He did the same with Way and Moses. "We have to go! Now! Government thugs could be here any second!"

"Why? What?" Allen fumbled with the blanket. He finally got his feet on the floor. "How do you know that? What's happening? What about the others? Thomas and Bart?"

Peter went back to Allen and leaned down, almost nose to nose with him. "Mom and Jack are up and ready. Thomas and Bart are taken care of."

Allen stopped. For a few seconds his mouth hung open. "'Taken care of'? What does that mean?"

"It means we don't have to worry about them, but we do have to go. I found some weapons stashed in Thomas's room. We'll take them with us. Mom and Jack are ready."

"Wait," Allen said. "You killed Thomas and Bart?"

"I explained it to all of you last night." Peter went to the window and moved the curtain, peeking outside. "I told you they were from the government. If we didn't deal with them, they were going to deal with us."

Allen stood and grabbed Peter. "You can't set yourself up as judge, jury, and executioner."

Peter stared outside, seeming to ignore Allen's grip. "It had to be done." He looked hard at Allen. "We couldn't just hang out with them and let them take us in, or kill us, or whatever they planned."

Allen released Peter and sat on the bed. "That's wrong. You shouldn't have done that. That's wrong."

Peter stood over Allen. He motioned toward Way and Moses. "We have them to take care of. Do you want the government to get them? The government catches them, they're dead. Plain and simple."

Way put on his shirt and slipped on his tennis shoes. He situated the sleeping Moses on the bed and started getting him ready.

"That's wrong." Allen shook his head. "There must have been some other way. Did you ever give them a chance to repent? Maybe they would have come in with us?"

Peter scoffed. "Seriously? Those guys were so deep in all that government brainwashing there was no hope for them."

"You're holding out hope for him." Allen poked a thumb toward Way.

"He had the sense to get out of the city to save his boy's life. Somehow the Lord was already working in him. He wouldn't have done that otherwise." Peter walked to the door. "Now, if you're going with us, get ready. If you want to stay here and sing 'Kumbaya' with the thugs when they get here, feel free. I guarantee they don't feel warm and fuzzy about you the way you seem to about them."

Allen grunted. "It's not that I feel warm and fuzzy about them. I just don't think it's our place to send them to Hell."

Way paused in getting Moses ready. "Where's Hell?"

Peter glanced out the window, then toward the doorway. "We don't have time to go into a lot of that. But it's that place of torment I told you about."

"What do Mom and Jack think about what you did?" Allen asked.

"They haven't had a chance to say much," Peter said, "but they sure didn't put up as much fuss as you have about getting out of here." He reached in his pants pocket and pulled out a scrap of cloth. He unfolded it, pulled out two grain-of-rice-sized computer chips and held them toward Way. "You were right about the chips. I got these out of their right hands. Do these things do as much as I figure they do?"

"Probably." Way took the chips and held them in his palm, examining them. "These tell their medical histories, their life histories even. Who their parents were. What Education Center they attended. Their education scores. Their heart rates, breathing rates, blood pressure, cholesterol levels, blood makeup, percentage of body fat, their domestic partners. About everything you would want to know about them, past and present, is contained on these. These chips also give their locations."

"So I'm right that that thing would tell that Group bunch these guys are dead?"

Way held the chips tight. "Oh, yes. The Group would have known the second their brain activity ceased and where it happened."

"You heard that, Allen." Peter opened the bedroom door. "I know you don't agree with what I did, but we can't discuss it now. We have to get out of here." He walked out.

Shaking, Way went back to getting Moses ready. "I try to stay out of your community's business and just follow along, and I understand you not liking what he did, but, trust me, you don't want The Group to get you. Remember, I've seen what they do to people who believe the way you do. It's horrible."

Allen buttoned his shirt. "I guess I'll go along for now, but I have some serious thinking to do."

Minutes later, Peter led Way and the others deeper into the woods.

There was no moon, no light, and Mom stumbled over a root. The others gathered around her, with Way holding Moses. Jack held Shamus by the fur on his neck.

As the others expressed their concern for Mom, Allen furrowed his brow and listened. "What's that? Do you all hear something?"

All the adults looked to the treetops and beyond.

"I hear something, but I don't see nothing," Jack said.

Whirring and buzzing filled the night air, replacing chirping crickets and croaking frogs as the dominant noises.

"Sounds like it's back that way." Peter jerked his head back toward the cabin.

As soon as those words were out of his mouth, there were several loud *zips* followed by a chain reaction of explosions. Flames rolled and stretched higher than the trees.

Jack removed his cap and clutched it to his chest. "Boss man, I think we're in trouble."

Peter tended to Mom's knee. "You could say that, yeah. Can you go, Mom?"

Mom reached for Peter to help her up. "I'll try for now, Brother Peter, but if I slow y'all down, you'll have to go without me."

"No. We'll never do that." Peter held her by one elbow.

Way grabbed the other elbow. "No. We can't do that."

Mom paused, blinked and stared at Way. "Well, thank you. I had no idea you felt that way."

Still holding Moses, Way gave one shoulder a slight raise. Moses played with Way's nose. Way moved the baby's hand. "That just wouldn't be right."

Peter slung a government rifle around his torso and started walking. "Let's go. We need to get as far away from here as fast as we can."

Way started after him. "About those weapons, it just occurred to me, they probably have chips in them so The Group can tell where they are."

Peter stopped and hung his head. "Aaargh!" He took the rifle from around himself and examined it. "You're probably right. I don't know why I didn't think of that." He grabbed the rifle by the barrel and slung it back toward the cabin. He took the other rifles and pistols one by one and slung them toward the cabin. Then he tossed the boxes of ammunition.

Way moved Moses's hand from his ear. "I hope you're not mad at me."

"No, not at all." Shaking his head, Peter bent and leaned on his knees. "I'm frustrated with myself and with those government thugs and the circumstances. This is nothing against you. You probably extended our lives by a good bit. I'm thankful that you thought of that and mentioned it. I was about to lead them right to us."

Jack patted Peter's back. "Don't worry about it, Pete. It could happen to any of us."

Peter stood. Sweat rolled down his forehead. "Thanks, Jack, but that was stupid on my part. I should've known better."

"Don't give it a second thought," Jack said. "It'll be all right."

The five adults took turns carrying Moses as they walked in thick woods over the next few hours. Shamus stayed close to Mountain Jack.

Way's stomach growled. It must have been about lunch time. They came to a creek.

"I'm beat." Peter sat on a fallen tree beside the water. "Let's rest a while and see if we can scare up something to eat."

"Sounds like a plan, boss man." Jack sat beside Peter. Shamus laid on the ground at Jack's feet.

"Here, let me help you with your gear." Allen assisted Mom in taking the pack from her back.

"Thank you," Mom said. She stretched. "That really is a load off."

"How's your leg?" Peter asked.

"All right." Mom took a few steps. "I don't know if I ought to sit down, though. I'm afraid it might stiffen up on me." She managed a smile. "Of course, I'm afraid that's the case with my whole, old body."

Way put Moses down. The toddler giggled and took several unsteady steps down the muddy creek bank toward the water. Way followed. He scanned the treetops. "Do you think The Group will send Corpsmen after us?"

Peter picked at the tree bark. He tossed a piece toward the creek. "Afraid so. It's not a matter of if, but when."

"I figure we need to spend as much time as possible under the trees." Jack pointed to the sky. "That at least gives us some covering and might kind of mess with their satellites and all their other gizmos."

"When they show up," Allen said, "I think we should surrender."

"Say what?" Jack's eyes widened.

"We should surrender." Allen shrugged. "We shouldn't do any more killing."

Peter rolled his eyes. "Here we go. If you feel that way, you should have stayed back at the cabin and let them pick you up. I'm sure some of their thugs have shown up there to look over the scene."

"When we were there, I didn't know this would be my decision. Now I believe it's the right thing to do. Killing's wrong."

Peter moved a piece of bark from one palm to the other and back again. "You do know there's times in the Bible that God called the people of Israel to fight, right?"

"That's Old Testament." Allen sighed. "We're in New Testament days now. It's peace, love, and forgiveness."

Moses plopped down at water's edge, reached into the creek and splashed several times.

Peter motioned to Way and Moses. "We still have these two to protect. I believe the Lord would have us help those who can't help themselves, and he would have us do that by every means possible. If someone's trying to kill them, or even you, Mom, or Jack, I believe the Lord would have me defend you with everything I have."

"Amen." Jack helped Shamus up beside him on the fallen tree. Shamus rested his chin on Jack's thigh.

Peter gestured, taking in the group. "Look at us. How many of us have they killed? My folks, my wife and kids, your folks, Mom's husband, Abe, Jack's wife and kids, all those they took from the cave not that long ago. They killed all those folks either directly or indirectly."

"Amen." Jack rubbed Shamus's head.

Allen glared at Jack. He rolled his tongue around in his mouth. "What about forgiveness?"

"What? Forgiveness?" Peter said.

"Yeah. What about turning the other cheek? What about forgiving others?"

Peter sat straight. "I'll kill 'em, then I'll forgive 'em."

Allen hung his head. He raised it back. "We've been in these woods a long time, but we're not animals."

Peter walked among his cohorts. "Right. We're not animals, but there's nothing wrong with us surviving. Look, we have a guy here who's not saved. We need to give him every opportunity to fix that. We have a boy here whose life depends on us. In fact, none of us can make it on our own. I believe it's okay in the Lord's eyes for me to try to stay alive, and for me to do everything I can to help all of you stay alive."

"Those men you killed back there, they weren't saved," Allen said. "The ones you're talking about killing to protect us, they're not saved either."

It was Peter's turn to hang his head. He closed his eyes and took in a deep breath. "Can't you understand? It's different. This isn't a live and let live situation. If all those unsaved ones you're talking about were just hanging around in the woods with us, it would be different. We could talk to them, witness to them, show them the love of God, tell them about Jesus, but that's not how it is. Those people are out to capture and kill us. They especially want Way and his boy, want them dead."

"Allen." Mom limped to Allen's side. "Much as I loved your mama and daddy and much as I love you, I got to go with Brother Peter here. I don't like the thought of sending them government men into eternity without them knowing the Lord, but I believe with everything in me the Lord let us cross paths with this young man and his boy so we could protect them."

Jack took off his cap and fidgeted with it. "I don't mean to dogpile here, Al, but I got to agree with Mom and Pete. We got to do everything we can to see Way and his boy through to salvation or freedom or something. We can't just let them thugs take them in. Nope, can't do it."

Moses picked up a rock and started to put it in his mouth. Way took it. He tossed it in the creek.

Mom chuckled. "Kids. Everything's always got to go to their mouths. My Abe was especially bad about that. Anything that wasn't tied down, was going straight to his mouth. Brother Peter, do you remember how he gnawed on everything he could get his mouth on when we all lived in the little cave where he was born?"

"I do. He ran around there with a constant string of dirt and slobber running out of his mouth."

Way wiped Moses's hands. "How did all of you end up out here? How did you make it without The Group providing for you?"

Peter picked up a flat rock. He brushed it against his pant leg. "I believe I told you a little of my story. When the government started taking guns from people, my dad decided it was time to get out of the city. No one was taking his guns. I was fourteen. We headed into the woods. Us and a bunch of others. We met Mom and her husband and their two oldest ones out here. My parents, them, and some others started kind of a little community. By and by, we met up with Mountain Jack, his wife, and their kids. They were part of a different little community, but the two bunches really became one, working together, helping each other." He skipped the rock across the creek.

"Impressive," Jack said.

"I still got it." Peter smiled and puffed out his chest.

"Didn't The Group come after you?" Way asked.

"They did some," Peter said. "Over the years, they'd come out in fits and starts, a little here, a lot there. They'd capture some, take them in, and those folks would never be heard from again." There was a catch in his voice. His eyes grew moist.

"Back in the day," Jack rubbed Shamus's head as he spoke, "there was near about fifty of us in our two connected bunches. Now you see what we're down to. It's like we're the last people on earth.

And, well, not to talk dirty in mixed company, if we don't find some females for you young fellows to marry up with, we're at the end of the road."

Way blinked. "'Marry up with'?"

"Yeah, you know, get hitched, enter into wedded bliss, jump the broom, drop anchor." Jack petted Shamus. He seemed to realize he wasn't getting anywhere. "Help me out here, folks."

Peter skipped another rock across the creek. "Good idea. Getting married, that's supposed to be a man and a woman loving each other, committing to live their lives together, and starting a family."

"Oh, we have something like that in the World Community." Way knelt beside Moses and brushed bits of mud and dead leaves out of the boy's hair. "We call them domestic partnerships. Two people: it doesn't have to be just a man and a woman, that's most common, but it's not limited to that, it can be two men or two women, sign an agreement to stay together for three years. When the time is up, they can either renew the partnership or they can end it." He paused and hung his head. "My partner, Luka, was going to end our partnership."

"Hold on, there, boy." Jack raised a finger. "The only thing wrong with all that stuff is, well, pretty much everything."

"What?"

Before Jack could speak, Peter stepped in. "That book I showed you, the Bible? In it, it says marriage is supposed to be between one man and one woman. People messed it up even before your Group came into power, but it sounds like they took it to a whole other level of messed up."

"Well, I wanted to continue my partnership with Luka, but she was going to end it. If one person wants to end it, that's all it takes. It ends."

Jack rested his cap on his thigh. "A messed up deal."

"I guess my Donald and me was married about twenty-five years before he passed away out here in these woods." Mom stared at Moses playing at creek's edge. "He passed when Abe was only about three. I wish that boy could've got to know his daddy."

Way looked at the other men in the group. "How about the rest of you."

Peter fiddled with his ear lobe. "My wife, Sandi, and I were married out here. Like I told you, I was fourteen when the world fell apart and Dad brought us out here. I met her out here. Being out of the city, folks out here, well, we got married by just standing before the Lord and having our leader take us through a ceremony of sorts. Your Group bunch wouldn't recognize it, but our people thought we had to do something kind of official. When we got married, it was one man and one woman for life. I believe, hope, the Lord looked on us as married. It was the best way we knew to keep some sort of order, some sort of society, going."

"For what it's worth," Mom said, "I believe in the Lord's eyes, you were just as married as if you'd had a big, fancy ceremony in the biggest, fanciest church in the world and signed all kinds of papers."

"Thank you," Peter said.

Jack offered a firm nod. "That goes for me, too, Pete."

Peter nodded back. "Thanks."

"Me, too," Allen said.

"Thanks. I appreciate that."

There was a lull in the conversation. Way took an unusual interest in his fingernails, then his feet, then the sky. He wanted someone to say something. He tried to think of something.

Jack broke the silence. "What say I scavenge around and find some fruit or something?"

Peter clapped. "Good idea. I'm hungry, and I'm sure our boy needs some groceries in him. While we're here, we need to fill our canteens."

Jack emptied his backpack. "Lord willing, I'll fill this thing up."

"Sounds good," Peter said. "You know, someone should go with you. I don't like one of us going too far out on their own."

"I'd probably be all right, but I got you." Jack threw a gesture toward Allen. "Come on, Al. Why don't you come with me unless you got something better to do?"

Chapter 14—Skipping Stones

The first several minutes after Jack and Allen left, silence reigned. Way concentrated on Moses. He was relieved to have his son there to give him something to concern himself with.

After sitting still for a time, Peter stood. He straightened his pant legs. He went to the creek's edge and picked up a couple of flat rocks. "Way, let me teach you to skip rocks."

Once Way was by his side, Peter started explaining what kind of rocks to look for, how to hold them, and the proper throwing motion.

"Before things fell apart, Dad would take me fishing," Peter said, "and after we'd fish for an hour or two, we almost always ended up skipping rocks. Dad was a pretty mean rock skipper." He eyed Way. "By 'mean,' I mean good." He looked from Way's eyes to the rock he'd given Way and back. "Give it a try."

Way drew back and threw. *Plunk!* The stone hit the water and went straight in, didn't skip once. He wrinkled his nose. "That wasn't so good."

Peter laughed. "You're right. That's okay, though. You'll get the hang of it."

Moses picked up a rock and tossed it in the creek.

"Lookie there," Mom said, "like father, like son. He wants to do what his daddy's doing."

Peter tilted his head toward Moses. "And that's why you need to be strong and do the right things in front of him. A boy needs a good dad, a man who'll teach him right from wrong and how to make his way in the world. A man who'll be there and be part of his life. Boys and girls both need a dad's good influence. Well, and a mom's, too."

"The Group says it knows best about raising offspring." Way felt the weight of the flat rock he held. He gave it a sidearm toss into the creek. It skipped twice. Way smiled. "The Group keeps children from seven in the morning until seven in the evening, and then it's lights out at ten, so the keepers only have the children awake three hours a day."

"'Keepers'? Is that what that Group bunch calls parents?" Peter asked.

Way scratched his head. "Well, yes. The Group says we keep them for their first five years, then The Group takes them, tests them and teaches them. The Group discovers what the offspring is good at and prepares them for their life task."

Peter skipped a rock. "Once the child turns five and that Group takes them, do the parents get to see them?"

"Oh, definitely, if they want to. The keepers can see the child for a three-hour visit the first Saturday evening of every month, if they desire."

Mom gasped. "Oh, dear."

"'Oh, dear' is right." Peter looked unhappy. "That's another area where your Group has it all wrong. The parents, they're not 'keepers,' should be the main influence in the child's life. They shouldn't just spend three hours a day with the child, much less three hours a month. They're the ones who should be nurturing the child, teaching them, helping them, providing for them. Somewhere along the line, the world got it all wrong. There's a philosophy, and I think it's right on, that whoever controls or influences a child when they are young will influence them their whole life. And I might add, in most cases, the parents should be the first to influence that child."

Moses picked up another rock and tossed it in the creek. He squealed.

Mom adjusted her glasses and put a finger to her chin. "You see, son, your Group wants to control everything. They want to keep their power. They think they can run things better than the good Lord. They want to control everything everyone does. They want to keep you under their thumb. Destroying the family, wiping out the natural affection of people for their parents leads them to not having natural affection for their children when those children come along. If you can destroy the family, you have a good start on destroying society, at least society the way it was meant to be."

"Good preaching." Peter pursed his lips.

Mom waved him off. "Oh, pshaw."

Way let Mom's words sink in before responding. "But The Group says it's there for our good. It helps us, takes care of us. The Group says the world was a mess before it came into power."

Peter scratched his head and raised an eyebrow. "Freedom can be messy. You let people make their own choices and sometimes they're going to make bad ones. You let people say what they think and sometimes they're going to say something that offends someone. It goes with the territory."

"Oh, The Group won't have that." Way shook his head. "No, that's one of the biggest crimes against the World Community. We are never to say anything offensive to or about another person."

"Your Group wants everyone to fall in line," Peter said. "They're happy as long as people are saying what they're supposed to say, believing what they're supposed to believe and doing what they're supposed to do."

Mom approached Way and with a light touch pressed her finger to his chest. "I know you don't understand all we're telling you, but I also know the good Lord put something in you, even with all those years of that Group brainwashing you. The Lord let you know you and that woman of yours should stay together. The Lord let you know it's wrong to kill that baby. I believe the Lord put it in your heart to get out of there."

Moses toddled into the water and plopped down. Water splashed in his face. He shivered and took in a deep breath. "Oooh."

"Cold, ain't it?" Peter laughed. He turned his attention to Way. "Think about what we tell you. Think hard. We want to help you even beyond right now." He paused and looked to the ground. "I don't say this a lot, but we love you and Moses and want to see you make it."

Way rocked from side to side. He wiped his eye. "Thank you."

"Yes, we do." Mom patted Way's shoulder. Smiling, she watched Moses sitting and splashing. "And I have to tell you, that boy of yours brings some much-needed light to our little world."

"He definitely does." Peter stepped into the creek and picked up Moses. "Don't you, buddy."

Moses squealed, wiggled, and grabbed Peter's ears.

Peter turned serious. "Mom, with it just being us three here, adult-wise, right now, what do you really think on the matter of killing those government thugs?"

With the serious turn the conversation took, Way figured it would be difficult for Peter to carry on with Moses grabbing his ears, so he took the baby.

Mom sighed. "Killing another person is a serious, serious thing, but I believe you're in the right."

"That means a lot coming from you," Peter said.

Mom waved him off. "Ah, I ain't nothing. I will say, though, when the Bible says 'Thou shalt not kill,' from what I heard back when we had regular church and regular preaching, it's talking about not killing innocent lives. Them men wasn't innocent, and the ones who'll come after us from now on ain't innocent." She tugged at the waistband of her pants. "Who knows how many people them men had killed or at least been a party to their deaths? I know taking another life, innocent or not, will weigh on you, but, under the circumstances, it had to be done."

Peter stared along the creek, into the distance. "It's good to hear that because I do wonder."

"I ain't much help, but I believe we need to do everything in our power to protect these two," Mom said.

About an hour later, Jack and Allen returned, and as Jack had hoped, the backpack was full. He poured out apples, grapes and blackberries.

Peter knelt on the ground beside the haul. "Good job." He picked up an apple and tossed and caught it a couple of times. He held it out to Mom. "All this should get us through a couple of days."

Moses went from the creek to the fruit.

"That boy knows it's lunchtime." Jack picked out a couple of grapes and gave them to Moses. They filled his palms.

"How'd it go for you guys?" Peter scrubbed an apple against his shirt.

Jack took off his cap and wiped sweat from his forehead. "Pretty good, I'd say. We was able to get some food, and we didn't run into no government goons, so I'd say it was a success."

"Any exciting discoveries?" Peter took a bite.

"Not really, other than a apple tree, some grape vines and a good berry patch." Jack put on his hat and snapped his fingers for Shamus to go to his side.

Allen popped a grape in his mouth. "Good and juicy."

"So, boss man," Jack rubbed Shamus's head, "what's our next move."

Peter swallowed a bite of apple. "I think our best move, even though it wouldn't be a surprise to the government at all, would be to head south. We can stay along the creek until it takes us to the river, then follow the river. I figure we can crisscross the creek and river, spend a few days on one side, a few days on the other, go south a few days, north a day or two. Just keep moving and make ourselves as hard as possible to track."

Mom studied the apple she held. "Long as we're farther south than north when winter hits. I can't take the cold like I used to. I don't know how my old bones will take another winter."

Jack stopped petting Shamus and eyed Peter. "That won't take us through Texas, will it? I vowed never to set foot in that wretched state after that year they beat us and kept us from an undefeated regular season."

Head down a bit, Peter cast a sideways glance at Jack. "Seriously? That was more than thirty years ago."

"I'm serious as a heart attack." Jack slapped his thigh. "I'm a man of principle. I held to that stand all this time, and I ain't breaking it now."

Peter smiled and took a bite of apple.

"I doubt there's even such a thing as Texas now," Allen said. "With this whole World Community and all, I don't think they even have states or anything anymore. Do they, Way?"

With a mouthful of apple, Way was caught off guard. He swallowed. "I don't even know what a Texas or a state is. All that you've said that is familiar to me is the World Community. We just all serve the World Community and The Group."

Jack slapped his thigh again. "Don't matter to me if there is or ain't a Texas. I ain't setting foot on any piece of ground that is, was, or could have been Texas. I got to stick to my guns on this."

Peter continued smiling. "Don't worry, Mountain. I'll see to it that we don't do anything to cause you to break your vow. Of course, you know, it's going to be hard to avoid every state that has a school that beat us."

Jack wiped his mouth. "It don't got to be every state, just Texas. Most times I dealt with losing pretty good, but that game was especially galling. We had a better team than them, and our boys played just awful that day. It was right there. We should have had it." He sighed. "Right there."

Way's confusion must have been evident.

Peter spoke to Way, but poked a thumb toward Jack. "That's probably part of the reason your Group outlawed sports. They make you crazy. People who are otherwise sane …," he paused and studied Jack, "well, mostly sane, lose their minds and become irrational over something they had no control over to start with."

"Tell me about it." Mom wiped apple juice on her pant leg. "My husband, bless his heart, he'd yell, 'Fumble!' and jump toward the TV like he was going to grab that ball before them boys that was standing two feet away from it could get it."

Peter chuckled. "Yeah, sports can sure make people do some crazy stuff. There were people who'd wear their lucky shirt or sit in their lucky chair to watch a game to help their team win like the shirt they wore or chair they sat in made a difference in a game." He scoffed.

Chapter 15—More Corpsmen

After everyone had their fill, the group members sat for a bit talking and watching Moses play.

Jack drifted into a mid-afternoon nap, with rhythmic snoring and an occasional mumble. Shamus slept at his side.

Moses squatted in ankle deep water and splashed. Allen crawled behind him and gave a playful roar. Moses stood straight and, laughing, toddled to Way. Allen followed and tugged at Moses's legs acting like he was trying to take him from Way's grasp.

Moses snuggled close in Way's lap. "Daa."

After several seconds, Allen backed away. More seconds passed and Moses, with a watchful eye on Allen, climbed from Way's lap and took a few apprehensive steps toward the creek.

Allen roared, and the laughing toddler hurried back to his dad. They repeated the scene several times. Everyone in the group, except the napping Jack, got a good laugh.

One last time, Moses ran laughing and squealing to Way. That time he climbed on Way, laid his head on his shoulder, and seemed ready to join Jack and Shamus for naptime.

Allen sat back and took a deep breath. "Did you and he play like that when you were in the city?"

Way palmed the back of Moses's head. "That kind of activity is frowned on by The Group. Sometimes, I would have a strong desire to get on the floor and roll around with him or interact with him in some other way, but Luka, my domestic partner, would chide me and remind me the cameras were on and that The Group could see everything we did."

"It's natural for you to want to play with him," Mom said. "Little ones need that sort of thing. It helps them know they're loved and helps them grow strong in body and mind."

Allen wiped his hair from his forehead. "As Jack would say your Group is full of something, and it ain't peaches and cream."

"They're right." Peter ran a stick across the flat stones. "That Group's whole agenda is to tear families apart and get people to look to them for everything."

"Think of this, son," Mom said, "if you had let them kill that boy, you wouldn't be enjoying this time with him now, playing with him, hearing him laugh, holding him."

Way closed his eyes a second. He stroked the back of Moses's head. "True." He waited. "Say, what would have happened to him if I had let them extinguish, … er, kill him?"

Mom stared into the distance. "Well, I believe, and I think all of us here believe about the same, that when a little one passes, they go to Heaven to be with Jesus."

Peter and Allen nodded.

"What does your Group say about the hereafter?" Mom asked.

"I take it you mean after one is extinguished?" Way said. "The Group allows everyone to make their own choice. We all choose our reality. The one thing we are not allowed is to believe that our religion is exclusive. The Group banned any branches of any religions that say they are the only way."

Peter widened his eyes and exhaled. "That's a problem. First, there can only be one reality. Second, Jesus said he's the only way to Heaven. When a man who rises from the dead says he's the only way someplace, I think it's a good idea to listen."

Mom adjusted her glasses. "On top of that, there was prophecy after prophecy that said Jesus was coming, who he was, and what he would do. There's also plenty of fulfilled prophecies about other things, to boot."

"So you say Jesus is the only way to get to Heaven?" Way swayed back and forth. "The Christians in the city say he's one of many ways."

"Well, the so-called Christians in the city compromise the truth." Peter's face reddened. The vein on his temple stood out. "They're deceivers. They don't believe the truth, and they're leading others down a path of destruction. Plain and simple." Peter dragged his pack to his side and pulled out the Bible. "Let me show you some of the things we're talking about."

Starting with John 3:16, Peter, Mom, and Allen shared passages with Way. The passages included Old Testament prophecies that Jesus fulfilled and New Testament claims of Jesus and his followers.

After about thirty minutes, Peter closed the Bible and put it back in his pack.

"And he loves me, huh?" Way said.

"You bet he does," Mom answered. "When he went to that cross we told you about, he went there for you just as much as he went for anyone. That Group of yours, it don't love you, it just wants what it can get out of you. It takes from you. God gives to you."

"Hmm." Way adjusted Moses to a more comfortable position. "That's interesting, definitely something to think about."

Peter latched the straps of his pack. "Remember, you don't have forever to make the choice. Thinking's fine, but there comes a time that you have to act on what you're thinking."

"I'll keep that in mind," Way said.

Jack snorted, waking himself. He rose to rest on his elbow. He blinked. "I must've dozed off. I miss anything?"

Jack's movement awakened Shamus. The dog stretched and yawned.

"You missed a good Bible study," Peter said.

Jack blinked hard and gave a quick head shake. "You should've woke me up. It's been too long since we had a good Bible study."

"True." Peter rubbed his thighs. "We probably need to start doing a little something every day. We could all use it."

"Boy, and talk about bringing a different perspective," Allen tilted his head toward Way, "I bet we'd really get a different perspective from Way."

Peter laid back, resting on his elbows. "Yeah, and hopefully, we could, with the Lord doing the work, of course, get some of that Group brainwashing out of his head."

Allen was sitting cross-legged next to Way. He patted Way's back. "I bet the Lord could do that. Opening blind eyes is one of his specialties."

Way furrowed his brow.

"It's a real thing, but in this case it's a figure of speech," Allen said. "We'll teach you. This is going to be good."

Peter bolted upright, looking south down the creek. He held a finger to his mouth. "Shh. Someone's down there."

Everyone sat still.

People downstream were talking.

Peter grabbed his pack. "Grab your stuff and get in the woods," he whispered.

As quick as they could, all of them had what they could carry and followed Peter's lead. Way, who held Moses, Jack, with Shamus by his side, and Allen ducked under the canopy of a thick, low-hanging willow. A few feet away, Peter and Mom sat behind a fallen tree.

A few minutes later, Way peeked between willow leaves. Three Corpsmen scoured the site he and the others had just left. They each wore a helmet. carried a rifle, wore a gun belt with two pistols each, and had a knife sheathed at their side.

"They were here not long ago," one of them said. His uniform had the most stripes on the sleeve. Way believed he was the leader. "They aren't far away. Spread out and search the area."

The Corpsmen put some distance between themselves as they left the creek bank and ventured into the woods.

The leader walked slower than the others and was more deliberate in his search.

Way thought his heart was going to pound out of his chest. He could hear it beating. Moses was still asleep.

Jack was kneeling next to Way. He hugged Shamus's neck.

On the other side of Jack, Allen knelt, eyes closed and lips moving. Way wasn't sure what he was doing.

From his vantage point, Way could see the tree Peter and Mom had ducked behind but couldn't see them.

The Corpsmen looked up and down and side to side. Although the two subordinates moved faster than the leader, they still seemed to take their time. One of them was several inches shorter and appeared several pounds lighter than the other.

The Corpsmen stepped closer and closer to the hiding places.

The leader stopped. He held his rifle in his left hand and rested his right hand on his holstered pistol. "They're in here somewhere. Our orders are to find them. The Group wants the runaway and the child alive. As for the rebels, we are not to leave these woods until we either have their dead bodies or have them in custody. And as if I need to remind you, if we extinguish them out here, there's less paperwork."

Way looked to the log where Peter and Mom hid. He saw occasional movement. Peter was doing something that caused him to move into a place where he could be seen. Way was sure the Corpsmen would be able to see him if they happened to look that way at the right time.

Peter peeked from behind the log. He held his knife high enough that Way could see it. When Peter saw that he had caught Way's eye, he jerked his head motioning for Way to get Jack's attention. Once Peter and Jack made eye contact, Peter motioned for Jack to get his bow and arrow ready. He signaled for Jack to take the bigger Corpsman. Peter pointed to his own throat, indicating where he wanted Jack to shoot his target.

Jack nodded and loaded his bow.

"No," Allen whispered. "No. You can't."

"Shh." Jack waved Allen off the best he could while holding his bow and arrow.

The two lower ranking Corpsmen seemed to catch wind of the activity. They made their way closer to the hidden rebels. They crouched and took one wary step after another.

Way saw that Peter had ducked behind the log. Jack drew back his bowstring.

The lower ranking Corpsmen were just steps away. It wouldn't be long until Way could grab the bigger one. The smaller one was closing in on the log that hid Peter and Mom.

Way managed to take his eyes off the Corpsmen and looked to Peter, who had him get Jack's attention.

Once he had that, Peter started counting down with his fingers while mouthing the words, "Three, ... two, ... one."

He stood and flung the knife, hitting the smaller Corpsman in the throat.

Jack let the arrow fly, and it found its mark.

The bigger Corpsman fell to his knees. He went face first to the ground.

The smaller one struggled for a couple of steps then crumpled.

The commander raised his wrist to his mouth. "Corpsmen under fire! Two Corpsmen down!"

He fired blindly in the direction of Way and the others.

"No!" Allen jumped up and ran to the smaller Corpsman.

Moses woke with a start, screaming and crying.

Jack grabbed another arrow, left the cover of the willow and hid behind an oak less than ten feet from Way.

The surviving Corpsman took cover behind a boulder.

Peter ran past the smaller Corpsman's body and grabbed his knife and the Corpsman's rifle. He joined Jack behind the oak.

Way stayed under the willow. He was on his knees, holding and rocking Moses. Mom was still behind the fallen tree.

Kneeling, Allen tried to tend to the smaller Corpsman. He removed the helmet. "It's a woman! She's dead! Peter, you killed a woman!"

"Allen, get out of there!" Peter said. "Move!"

"No! You killed a woman!"

"There's no way out." The ranking Corpsman was still behind the boulder. "In minutes, the area will be filled with drones and Corpsmen. You have no hope of escape. Throw down your weapons and come out. The easier you make this now, the easier we'll take it on you when we get you to the city."

"That's a lie!" Peter said. "Just like everything else your Group says, you're lying!"

Way could see Peter's hair was wet with sweat. Jack was on the other side of Peter, to his right.

"No. It's not a lie," the Corpsman said. "The Group will give you a chance to rehabilitate. You'll have a chance to get right with The Group. No more of you have to die."

Peter breathed hard. "If you haven't noticed, you're the one who's outnumbered here and none of us have died. You're the one who's losing people. What will your Group say about that?"

"The Group understands. It knows what we're dealing with. Here's a deal for you. All you have to do is give us the runaway and the offspring. The rest of you can go free."

"You're not taking any of us," Peter said. "Way and his son are with us now. We're not going anywhere without them."

Allen stood. "How about me? Would you take me in his place?"

"Get down, you idiot!" Peter said.

The Corpsman raised, peeking over the boulder. "You would turn yourself in to save the runaway?"

"Yes. Take me." Allen walked toward the boulder.

"Allen, stop!" Peter called.

"No. I have to do this."

"He's the only one of you showing any sense." The Corpsman continued to peek over the boulder. "Come on. The Group will appreciate your willingness to cooperate."

"Allen, stop!"

"I have to, Peter."

"That's it. Keep coming," The Corpsman motioned Allen closer.

Allen took several more steps.

"There you go," the Corpsman spoke in slow, measured tones. "Keep coming."

"You see. It has to be this way." Allen kept walking. "It's all right. This is the right thing."

"Yes, it is," the Corpsman said. "Come on."

Allen kept walking. "I need to do this."

"Yes, you do," the Corpsman said.

He stood, took aim, and fired. Allen whirled and fell.

A second shot rang, the Corpsman stumbled back and fell into the creek.

Peter tossed the female Corpsman's rifle to the side. "You all take care of Allen. I'll check on the thug," he said as he ran.

Mom and Jack, with Shamus at his side, ran to Allen. Way left the cover of the willow, but hung back, still holding the crying Moses.

Mom raised Allen's head. "You're going to be all right, son. He got you in the arm. Brother Jack, see if any of them thugs has a first aid kit on them. If they do, bring it here. If they don't, tear off a piece of their clothes. We'll use it for a bandage."

Tearing through the male Corpsman's backpack, Jack found a small first aid kit.

Peter returned to the others. "Dead. We have to go, fast. That Group and its people lie about most everything, but I believe he was telling the truth about drones and thugs coming."

"We're going to fix you up." Mom cut Allen's shirt sleeve and wrapped gauze around his wound. "The bullet went through, so at least we don't have to worry about getting it out. And, by the grace of God, it didn't hit your bone. That would've been a mess."

Peter tossed away the female Corpsman's rifle. "That thing probably has a chip in it that would lead them right to us. We have to go. You ready to run, Allen?"

Allen propped himself up on his elbows. "Why don't I just stay here and let them get me? Maybe that would at least slow them down on chasing you all."

"We're all together." Peter stooped and took hold of Allen. "Let's go. We can't leave you. That wasn't the brightest move you've ever made, but we still need you with us."

Allen stood. He took a few seconds to stop swaying. "I thought it would help." He looked hard at Peter. "You killed a woman."

Peter surveyed the treetops. "We don't have time to go into it, but yes, I did. Two things on that, though. First, I didn't know she was a woman when I killed her, and, second, it was a woman who planned to kill us."

"I don't know, killing a woman." Allen slumped his shoulders.

Peter grabbed Allen and started walking. "We don't have time. This place is going to be crawling with thugs and drones in just a few minutes. We have to go." He looked to the others. "Grab as much as you can, we have to go."

Chapter 16—Fire

About ten minutes later Way and the others had managed to get about half a mile away from the site where the run-in with the Corpsmen took place. The woods thickened. A woodpecker pounded on a nearby tree, looking for food.

Shamus's ears perked up. He whimpered.

"What is it, boy?" Jack rubbed Shamus's neck.

"Listen." Peter put his fingers to his ear. He looked back in the direction from which they had come. "Look."

Under the covering of the trees, only bits and pieces of the sky were visible, but Way saw enough to see five black helicopters circling near the area they had left.

Next there was a great *whirring*.

Jack covered his ears. "That sounds like a swarm of locusts."

Shamus whined and pawed at the ground.

Dozens of drones flew in different directions from where the rebels had been.

"What we going to do, boss man?" Jack still covered his ears. "Looks like it's getting serious."

"It's big trouble," Peter called over the din. "Don't anyone get under open sky. We have to find a place to hide."

Allen covered his wound. "Another reason we shouldn't have been killing."

Peter stopped and glared. "Everyone try to stay together. We won't split up unless we have to."

A flock of sparrows flew past going away from the helicopters and drones. A rabbit ran across Mom's toes in the same direction the sparrows flew.

Mom jumped. "Well, I never."

Way bounced the screaming Moses on his hip. He pointed up a hill. "How about up there."

About halfway up the hill was a thicket of bushes.

Peter started toward it. "Good job. That's the best we have right now. Let's hurry." He took Moses from Way. "I'll get him for now. You just hurry up there."

Way hesitated.

Peter gave a firm, quick nod. "I got him. He'll be all right."

The hill was so steep Way had to get on all fours to climb. He noticed Peter held Moses and still managed to claw his way up.

They reached the thicket and struggled through the stickers, vines, and branches to hide.

Once inside, Jack and Mom sat. Shamus stood by Jack. He nuzzled his snout into Jack's neck. Peter gave Moses to Way.

Jack held Shamus close. "It looks dark, don't it, boss man?"

Peter bent at the waist and peered out of the thicket. "It's looked better."

Allen went to one knee. He put his fingers to his chin. "Peter, it's obvious your way isn't working. I say we stop the killing, turn ourselves in, and ask for mercy."

"I usually don't say much," Way said, "but The Group doesn't show mercy. I've seen dozens of people ask for mercy when The Group tries to rehabilitate them. It never works. They get it just as bad as those who are defiant to the end."

Peter stood straight. "There it is. You heard it from someone who's seen it. They don't show mercy. They just kill anyone who doesn't agree with them."

"Isn't that what you're doing?" Allen asked. "Killing people who don't agree with you?"

Peter closed his eyes and took in a breath. "I've killed people who are trying to kill my friends. I've killed people who want me to denounce Jesus." He poked a thumb toward Way. "I've killed people who are trying to kill a friend, who as far as I know, hasn't accepted Jesus as Savior yet. I've killed people who want to kill his baby boy."

"What about turning the other cheek?"

Peter slumped his shoulders. "Look, we've gone around and around on this for weeks now. You think what you want to think, I think what I want to think. I don't believe we're ever going to agree." He paused. "I love you, man, but I just don't think we're ever going to come to terms on this. I just ask that you go along with us and help keep Way and Moses safe."

"That sounds like good sense to me." Jack slapped a knee. "You all been chasing that squirrel around the tree long enough. I believe you can both point to cases in the Bible that support your arguments. You all are going to have to let Jesus sort it out when you meet up with him, which, I'm afraid from the looks of it, may not be too long. Time to let it go and take care of the most immediate concern, which I believe is helping ol' Way and his boy out of their predicament."

"I'll agree to that," Mom said.

Peter lowered his gaze. He clicked his tongue. "Jack and Mom are right. We need to set aside these arguments and take care of Way. By the way, I apologize for calling you an idiot back there. I shouldn't have done that. I'm embarrassed by the way I acted." He reached out to Allen.

Allen stood and looked at Peter's hand. He didn't take it. "Does that mean you still kill people?"

Peter exhaled. He rubbed the back of his neck. "If it comes to it, yeah, I guess so."

A helicopter flew over them.

Allen raised his eyebrows and sighed. "Then I can't shake. I can't go along with killing, no matter the reason." He looked at Way. "I'm sorry. It's nothing at all against you or Moses. I just don't believe in taking a person's life." He blinked hard. His eyes moistened. "I love all of you. You've been my family for years and years, but I have to go." He took a step to leave the thicket.

"Allen, wait." Peter clutched Allen's arm.

"I have to. I accept your apology, and I love you like a brother, but I have to go." With a gentle tug, Allen pulled away from Peter's grip. "I won't give you all away, but I have to go. God be with you." He turned and left the thicket.

Mom and Jack stood. They joined Way and Peter in peeking out of the thicket.

Allen walked toward a Corpsman about a hundred yards from the thicket.

In the thicket, Peter spoke through gritted teeth. "Allen, what are you doing?"

Jack rubbed Shamus's neck. "Thirty years of surviving in the woods for it to end this way for him. I don't get that boy."

The Corpsman called some of his cohorts and motioned them to him. Several Corpsmen gathered around Allen.

The first Corpsman stepped and punched Allen in the stomach, doubling him over. He gave him an uppercut to the face.

The other Corpsmen laughed.

The first Corpsman shoved Allen. Allen stumbled back a few feet and fell.

Watching from the thicket, Way winced.

"Jesus, help him," Mom said.

The Corpsmen gathered around Allen. They beat him with clubs and kicked him. Allen curled into a ball.

A couple of Corpsmen grabbed Allen. They dragged him toward their original landing site. Several laughing Corpsmen trailed after.

Jack removed his hat and scratched his head. "What now, boss man?"

Exhaling, Peter ran his fingers through his hair. "I believe our best bet is to wait here. The more we move around, the more chance there is that they find us."

"So sometimes it's better to move and sometimes it's better to stay still?" Way still held Moses.

"That's about it," Peter said.

After about thirty minutes the Corpsmen moved on. The helicopters thinned out.

Way was sitting cross-legged in the thicket. He kept Moses, who was playing in the dirt, within a couple of feet. "Maybe I should turn myself in. I've been nothing but trouble since you found me. You've lost several friends and family because of Moses and me."

"You'll do no such thing." Mom pointed a crooked finger.

"But—"

Mom cut him off. "Far as I know you haven't give your life to Jesus. That's the most important thing a person can ever do, give their life to Jesus. Once them goons get hold of you, it's over for you. Your life on this earth is done. Once your life on this earth is done, your eternal destiny is set. At that point, it's either Heaven and a perfect world, or Hell and everlasting punishment."

Way toyed with a small stick. "But I don't understand."

Mom patted Way's knee. "You don't have to understand it all. You have any questions, you can ask any of us. We'll help you the best we can. You keep thinking, but remember, you're not guaranteed even one more second. That's not to scare you or force you to accept Jesus, it's just a cold, hard fact. After you're dead, it's too late."

Peter stood and stretched. "Oh, boy, I'd stretch a mile if I didn't have to walk back." He ambled to the bushes and peered out. "It's calmed down out there. Maybe they'll leave us alone for a while. Let's get a little rest, then we'll move out after dark."

Using a broken limb as a headrest, Jack laid down. He pulled his John Deere cap over his eyes. "Sounds like a plan, boss man."

"Wake up." Peter jostled Way.

Way blinked a couple of times. It was dark.

Peter stood. "We're going to head out."

Jack picked up Moses. "I'll carry ol' Mo here. Me and him need to get better acquainted."

Moses tugged on Jack's beard.

Jack poked Moses in the stomach. "Boy, you want me to drive you a-bug hunting?"

Moses squealed and shielded his stomach from Jack's tickling.

About fifteen minutes after Way and the others left the thicket the familiar *whirr* of drones came from the area they had left.

"Oh, no," Peter groaned.

"Here we go again, Pete." Jack still carried Moses, who had taken Jack's cap and placed it on his own head.

"Yeah, here we go again."

A whistle was followed by an explosion. Then another. And another. And another.

Fire lit the sky behind the rebels.

Shamus barked.

"We have to find shelter!" Peter started running. He ran slow enough, though, that Jack and Mom could keep up. Shamus ran beside Jack.

Even with their advanced years, Jack and Mom seemed to keep pace better than Way. His lungs and thighs burned. It didn't take long for his legs to feel like gel. He huffed.

Peter looked over his shoulders and noticed Way's struggle. He stepped aside to let Jack and Mom pass. He moved alongside Way. "Come on, man. You can do it. This is for Moses."

Way nodded. The woods spun around him.

Whistle. Whistle. Whistle.

Boom. Boom. Boom.

The ground trembled under the rebels. Way looked back. The fire grew.

Sweat rolled into Way's eyes. He couldn't breathe. He didn't know what it was like to drown, but thought it must be like what he felt at that time. He stumbled, but Peter kept him from falling.

Mom spotted something. "Over here!" She waved for the others to follow her.

The w*histles* and *booms* drew closer.

Mom led them to the face of a short cliff. The adults sat and pressed their backs hard against the face. Shamus growled and barked at the commotion.

Jack held tight to the crying Moses. "I got you, little fellow. I got you. It's okay."

They all huddled together. Mom raised her forearm to shield her face.

Way watched as the explosions got closer. Closer. Closer.

The fire in the distance grew.

Way felt the heat from it and from the explosions.

"What do we do, boss man?" Jack called.

Peter wiped sweat from his forehead. In the process he smeared a couple of dirt streaks "Wait and pray, brother. Wait and pray."

The explosions grew more sporadic. Thirty seconds or so passed between strikes. A minute. Two minutes. Finally, it had been about fifteen minutes with no drones, no explosions. The fire died.

Moses calmed. Shamus calmed.

Way bent and reached toward Moses, who was sitting on Jack's lap. "Come here, boy."

Moses wallowed off of Jack's lap and toddled to Way, giggling. "Da!"

Smiling, Jack retrieved his cap from the ground where Moses had dropped it. "Oh, sure, leave me." He sniffed and wrinkled his nose. "Man, it smells like the mother of all campfires out here. I ain't ever going to get the stink of smoke out of my beard."

"What do we do now, Brother Peter?" Mom asked.

Peter had a loose grip on his knife handle. "You know, I think we should backtrack. Let's give them some time to clear out, then go back to where those last thugs found us. Maybe they expect us to get as far from here as we can."

Jack slapped his cap against his thigh. Dust flew. "Sounds like a plan. That's why you're the boss man."

Chapter 17—Camp

Several hours later, with only the moon to light the area, the rebels were back at the creek where they had encountered the three Corpsmen. Haze hung in the air from explosions and fire.

Their gear was where they'd left it when they left the creek bank.

"We might as well get our stuff in order." Peter stooped to pick up his canteen.

Jack took stock of his supplies. "So you figure for us to stay around here for a spell?"

Rubbing his chin, Peter surveyed the scene. "That might be good. Like I said, maybe they'll look for us to be on the move away from this area. I don't know. What do you all think?"

Jack adjusted his cap. "That makes sense. At this point, it sounds as good as anything else."

"I agree," Mom said. "It's a little scary to stay here where they found us, but it might be the best place."

"What do you think, Way?" Peter asked. "You know more about that Group bunch and those Corpsmen than any of us. What do you think?"

Way followed Moses to the creek. "I know a little about them, apparently not everything I thought I knew is true, but what you propose makes sense."

"I guess you see they're pretty serious about getting you and your boy." Peter slung his pack over his back.

Way huffed. "I kind of put that together."

Jack planted both feet. "They'll do that over my dead body."

"Mine, too," Peter said.

"And mine," Mom said.

Way wiped his eyes. "You have no idea what that means to me. All you've done for us, I just can't ..."

Peter patted Way's back. "Don't worry about it. Given the same opportunity, you'd do the same for any of us."

"Maybe." Way raised his shoulders. "I hope so. I don't know. In the city everyone worries about themselves, following the rules, doing what The Group says. World citizens report each other for the simplest violations. Back there, it's a violation to know about a violation and not report it."

"Even your wife would report you if you broke one of their rules?" Jack asked.

"If you mean Luka, my domestic partner, oh, yes, in a heartbeat. She is a stickler for the rules, follows them down to the letter. Of course, her desire is to move up the ranks, so she wants to look as good as she can to The Group."

Jack clicked his tongue. "What a world we got."

Mom worked to set up something of a camp. "Terrible. Mamas who'll let their babies be killed so they won't be inconvenienced. I would say I never thought I'd see the day, but the Bible told us it was coming."

Peter pulled his Bible out of his backpack. "Mom, if you can hold off on setting up camp for a bit, this might be a good time for a little Bible study."

Mom set down the sticks she had gathered and wiped away the dirt and grit on her pant legs. "Sure, Brother Peter. There's always time for that."

"Jack, could you get a fire going to give us a little light?" Peter asked.

"And give us a little heat, too." Mom hugged herself.

After Jack got the fire going, the adults gathered around it. Moses was asleep next to Way. Shamus laid beside Jack.

Peter sat cross-legged and thumbed through the Bible. "Let's see, I believe what I'm looking for is in Second Timothy. Hmm." He ran his finger along the pages. "Yep, here it is, chapter three, starting at verse one. 'This know also, that in the last days perilous times shall come. For men shall be lovers of their own selves, covetous, boasters, proud, blasphemers, disobedient to parents, unthankful, unholy, without natural affection, trucebreakers, false accusers, incontinent, fierce, despisers of those that are good, traitors, heady, high-minded, lovers of pleasures more than lovers of God; having a form of godliness but denying the power thereof: from such turn away.'

"I want to go over all of this, but to start with, let's hit on this 'without natural affection' thing."

Peter started the discussion, and soon Mom and Jack were adding their thoughts. Way did his best to follow.

After about thirty minutes, Peter closed the Bible. "I know we hit you with a lot of stuff there, Way, but in a nutshell, this passage hits on just about everything your Group stands for and wants out of people."

Way pinched his chin. He pursed his lips. "And you say that was written about two thousand years ago? From the way you three explained it, it's almost like the writer was here now, watching."

"That's God for you," Peter said. "He led a man named Paul to write this way back yonder, knowing that this time was coming and trying to warn and prepare folks for it."

Mom adjusted her glasses. "You see, son, the way you talked about wanting to roll around on the floor and play with your boy, that's natural affection. The way you want to keep him alive, that's natural affection. That woman of yours wanting to have him killed, that's not the way the Lord made us. That goes against everything God designed mamas and daddies to be, but I'm afraid that's where the world has gone."

Way awakened just after sunrise the next morning holding Moses close. The baby was snuggled with his head at Way's shoulder. Way's back was to Peter and Jack, and they were talking.

"What do you figure our chances are of getting out of this alive?" Jack asked.

"Don't know," Peter said. "Not good, but even in the best of circumstances you're never going to get out of life alive. Isn't that right?"

Jack grunted. "True. I just hope we can accomplish what we need to with the boy there before we run out of time."

"The Lord's working. Way's interested. I think he's come a long way in the short time he's been with us. He's a good-hearted guy. Under what used to be normal circumstances, he probably would've given his life to the Lord long ago. You can't ever tell. I've known people who sat in church Sunday after Sunday, year after year, and then when they're on their deathbed you still don't know where they're going to end up. They heard enough preaching to save millions of people, but it never cracked their heart."

"Yep. I knowed a few like that myself."

"With Way, what'd he say, he's like twenty-four? We're trying to break through twenty-four years of brainwashing and indoctrination. It's not going to happen overnight, or, apparently, even in a few weeks."

"You're right. Like you said, he's a good kid. It shows a lot that he wants to keep his boy alive bad enough that he was willing to make his escape. That was a brave thing, took a lot of backbone."

Way heard rustling.

"Why didn't you boys wake me up?" Mom asked.

"Figured you could use some rest," Peter said. "I thought we'd let you sleep as long as you needed."

"Oh, I should've been up hours ago. This ain't no time for sleeping your life away." Mom apparently noticed Way still under his blanket. "Except him. That boy's got the weight of the world on him. This has to be a great stress and strain on him. The rest of us been out here all these years and know what it's like dodging them government thugs. But him, everything he knows has been turned upside down these last few weeks." Mom's voice cracked. "I sure do love that boy and his boy. Wish I'd got the chance to know him as a little one."

"You wish you could've raised him from a pup?" Jack laughed.

Mom chuckled. "I guess I do. That would've been nice."

Way felt a warmth come over him like a blanket. He couldn't help but smile. He couldn't lay there anymore not speaking. With great care, he laid Moses's head on the pallet. He sat up. "Thank you. I didn't mean to be rude, but I heard what you said, Mom. Thank you. I wish I could've known you when I was little. I don't remember my father and mother. All I remember is being moved to the Regional Education Center full-time when I was five, and The Group teaching us its ways. I ... I don't remember anything before that."

Jack tugged the bill of his cap. "Boy, they messed you up good. Well, I reckon they messed everyone up good." He patted Way. "In fact, maybe they didn't mess you up. You're one of the few that seems to have made it through all this Group business with some sense in your head."

Peter studied his fingernails. "So knowing that your boy could be killed on his first birthday or that he would eventually be taken from you and raised by that Group, why did you and your wife have him in the first place?"

Way watched Moses sleep. "I don't know. There was just something in me that wanted an offspring, for better or worse. I guess I hoped things would change and somehow I'd get to see him

148

grow. I had to talk Luka into having him. She never wanted him. Having him was the only thing that she ever relented to me on." He sighed. "I guess it shouldn't have surprised me when she wanted him extinguished, er, killed."

"Bud, are you sorry you ran away from that prison?" Jack hooked a thumb around his overall strap.

"Prison?"

"Whether you knew it or anyone else knew it, they had you in prison. With that bunch, everyone but the most higher ups is in prison."

Way scoffed. "You're right. I'd never thought of it that way. That's not the way The Group tells it. The Group tells us how free we are and how good we have it."

Jack chuckled. "That's what them female spiders do just before they eat their mates."

Way wrinkled his nose.

"It's ugly, but, yeah. The way I hear it, some spiders, they mate and then," Jack ran a finger across the front of his throat, "kkkk, the female eats the male."

Way's eyes opened wide. "The Group didn't teach me that. Anyway, back to your question. I'm not sorry I ran away. I am sorry for the trouble I've caused all of you, but I'm not sorry I ran away." He rubbed Moses's hair. "However long it lasts, I'm glad for the time I've had with Moses, and I'm glad to have met all of you. You've shown me a side of people and life that I didn't see in the city."

Peter sat on his haunches. "I believe we've told you, but I don't think we can tell you enough, we're glad to have you."

"I'm sorry to break up this talk, but my belly's snarling at me, letting me know it wants filled." Jack palmed his stomach.

Peter dumped a rock from one palm to the other and back again. "It would be a good idea to get some breakfast. Jack, would you mind seeing if you can scare up some berries or something?"

"Glad to." Jack stood. "Way, you want to come along? Maybe Mom and Pete can watch your boy for you."

Way looked from Mom to Peter.

"Fine with me," Peter said.

"Me, too," Mom said.

The next few days passed slowly. Way and the others stayed along the creek. Jack and Way made daily trips to gather food, whether by picking fruits and vegetables or catching an occasional squirrel or rabbit. Jack's fishing pole proved useful at the creek and at a nearby pond. And the pond attracted ducks that proved to be a treat for the rebels.

Jack and Peter had built a fire, and Peter kept it going with help from the others. They put a covering, consisting of an old blanket tied to four small logs, over the fire in hopes that would make it difficult for The Group's satellites to detect.

Moses found plenty to do wandering here and there, exploring.

They had put together three lean-tos, one for Way and Moses, one for Jack and Peter, and one for Mom. They settled in the best they could not knowing when they would have to run or hide again.

Chapter 18—Wandering

Peter popped a lunchtime blackberry in his mouth. "Thanks again for lunch, Jack, Way. You guys have fed us pretty good the last few days."

"You're welcome," Way said.

"Welcome," Jack said through a mouthful of his own blackberries.

Mom gave Moses a couple of blackberries. "Here you go, boy. Maybe these will give you enough energy to make it through the day."

Jack scoffed. "I'm afraid we're the ones that need the energy. We have to keep up with him."

"How'd you and your wife keep that little fellow penned up in your house without him going stir crazy and driving you crazy to boot?" Peter asked.

Way swallowed a blackberry. "He hadn't been crawling or walking long, so we hadn't really got into him being too active. Luka kept all the doors in the pod closed to keep him in one room. And The Group helps manage offspring by giving them a special diet that keeps their energy level down."

Jack scoffed again. "Yeah, they probably drug the little ones to high heaven."

Way tilted his head and raised a shoulder. "I don't know what 'high heaven' is, but The Group supplements an offspring's diet in an effort to keep them from being hyperactive."

"From being normal, you mean," Jack said.

"The Group just knows that parents in the World Community have to focus more on their tasks and less on the offspring. An offspring that's too active takes too much of the parent's energy. The Group helps with that."

Jack shook his head. "That bunch helps with a lot of things, mostly with the ruination of the world."

Peter watched a blue jay fly from a tree to the ground. It scratched in the dirt a few seconds, then flew back to the tree. "I'd say Jack hit it about right. Their 'help' is more to help them than anyone else. They want to control everyone and everything. We came out here to get away from them, and they can't stand it. We just want to be left alone, mind our own business, and do our own thing, and they won't let that happen."

"It's got more intense these last few weeks, but, yeah, all along, they haven't liked us." Jack adjusted his cap.

"But the Lord's going to see us through someway, somehow," Mom said.

Jack waved his cap. "Whoo-hoo! That he is, Mom. That he is. I can't hardly wait to see how he takes care of this whole situation. I know it's going to be good."

"But what if it ends with all of us being captured and tortured?" Way asked.

"That will definitely be rough," Peter interlocked his fingers, "but there's a place in the Bible where it talks about Jesus's followers rejoicing because they were worthy to suffer shame for him. I guess we'll do the same."

"Besides that, boy, whatever they put us through is temporary, no matter how long it lasts," Jack said. "It'll end. Eternity, what we have waiting for us on the other side of that torture, will go forever. As bad as what they put us through is, it's nothing compared to how great Heaven is for those who believe."

"Well said." Peter offered a firm nod.

Way gazed down the creek. "Interesting. And you're sure of that?"

"Sure as I can be of anything." Jack shivered. "All the way down to my bones."

Mom poked Way. "I'm more sure of that than I am that you're standing right in front of me. And when I get there, I'll get to see my Abe again and my husband, Donald, and my two oldest kids." Mom's eyes glistened. "That'll be the day. There's an old song by the name of 'What a Day That Will Be,' that pretty well says it all. It will be so great to see Jesus and all my loved ones that's gone on before."

Peter kept watching the blue jay. "Our puny little minds can't even grasp how great it's going to be."

"Amen to that, brother." Jack rocked back and forth.

Way gave Moses a blackberry. "That will be nice if it's all as you believe."

Jack took off his cap, and closed one eye as he scratched his head. "There's a catch, bud."

"Oh, yeah?"

"Yeah, afraid so."

"And what's that?"

Jack sucked air through clenched teeth and raised his shoulders. "Far as I can tell, as it stands right now, you ain't going."

"Brother Jack!" Mom sounded like she was scolding a child.

Head forward, Jack scratched his head again. "I don't know no other way to tell it than just like it is."

"You could be a little easier about it." Mom's face grew redder by the second.

Peter stepped in. He smiled and looked Way in the eye. "Jack's about as subtle as a charging rhinoceros." He chuckled. "But what he's getting at is as true as it gets." He motioned toward his backpack laying a few feet away. "That Bible in there says the only way to get to Heaven is to accept Jesus as your Savior. We have to admit that we're sinners, believe he's the Son of God and confess with our mouths that he is Lord."

Way looked into the distance. "Like I've told you before, The Group says we can believe whatever we want, as long as we don't push our beliefs on others."

Peter squinted and put a finger to his temple. "I'm afraid getting spiritual guidance from that bunch is like taking flying lessons from a rock. It ain't going to get you anywhere good."

Scuffing at some rocks with one foot, Way took a deep breath. "You've given me more to think about."

"Think hard, bud. Think hard," Jack said.

Way woke the next morning. There was an empty spot at his shoulder where Moses normally slept. Way felt. No Moses. Way sat. His heart raced. His stomach knotted. Still sitting, he took a hurried look around camp. No Moses. Way shot to his feet.

Peter and Jack, Way thought. He looked in their lean-to. There they were. No Moses.

Mom. He looked. Sound asleep. No Moses.

The creek, Moses's favorite place. Nothing.

"Moses! Moses!"

Way's yells woke the others.

Jack blinked hard. "What's going on, bud?"

"What is it?" Peter asked.

"Moses. I can't find Moses." Way clutched his hair. "He was here when I went to sleep, just like usual. Now he's gone. I can't find him."

"Oh, Jesus, help us." Mom hurried from one spot to another to another to another.

Peter moved to Way and patted his back. "Calm down. He can't have gone far. We'll find him."

"How could I let him get away?" Way was weak-kneed. "Why didn't I feel him move?"

"Don't worry, bud. Don't worry. We got this." Jack gathered his gear.

"Mom," Peter said, "you mind staying here while we look for the baby? You know, just in case he shows up back here."

Mom wrung her gnarled fingers. "I'd rather be moving and doing something, but yes, I understand. I'll stay here."

Jack hung his canteen over his shoulder and across his chest. "You can definitely pray. That's the best thing any of us can do right now, and you can touch the Lord with the best of them."

"Jack, let's split up." Peter said a few minutes into the search. He pointed to the north. "You and Shamus go that way. Way and I will go south. Let's keep it fairly close around here. I really doubt he's gone far. And keep your ears open. He's probably chattering away out here, thinking he's having a big time playing and exploring."

"Got you, boss man." Jack doffed his cap. He turned his attention to Way. "Don't worry, son, me and Pete know our way around the woods pretty good. We'll find that boy."

Way managed a feeble nod.

Just a couple of minutes after leaving Jack, Way heard voices.

Peter stopped. He heard them, too. He held a finger to his lips.

Way listened. It wasn't Jack. It wasn't a chattering Moses. Way definitely heard two adult men.

Peter led Way into a thicket. They peered in the direction of the voices. About a city block away, two Corpsmen made their way through the woods.

"Great," Peter whispered. "It's some of them. Not only do we have to avoid them, but we have to find Moses before they do."

Way had thought his stomach could not be any more knotted. He found out different.

"Moses! Mo!" Jack called from the opposite direction.

The Corpsmen stopped. They faced the direction of Jack's voice.

Peter's shoulders drooped. He hung his head.

Way's heart sank.

"Mo! Where you at, boy?" Jack called.

The Corpsmen walked in Jack's direction.

"That's definitely one of them," one of the Corpsmen said.

Each of the Corpsmen had a rifle, a holstered pistol, and a knife.

They stalked through the woods, like snakes slithering toward unsuspecting prey.

"Mo! Where you at? Come out, come out, wherever you are!"

Peter hung his head and rubbed his forehead. "Lord, please shut him up."

Jack cackled. "Ah, there you are! Boy, is your daddy going to be glad to see you! Wait 'til we find him and Pete."

The Corpsmen stopped and looked at each other a second, then continued. They neared the thicket. A few steps away. Closer. Closer.

Way could have grabbed one of them by the nose. It seemed he could feel their breath.

They passed.

Still unaware of the Corpsmen, Jack continued talking to Moses.

Peter pounced from the thicket. He grabbed a Corpsman by the head and twisted. Way heard the snap. The Corpsman collapsed, dead.

The other Corpsman wheeled with rifle upraised and ready to shoot. Way bounded out of the thicket and drove his shoulder into the Corpsman's midsection, tackling him. An errant round of shots fired.

Peter drove his knife into the Corpsman's throat.

Wide-eyed, the Corpsman gurgled, struggling to breathe. He stopped. There was no more breath, no more heartbeat.

A radio crackled. "Seventeen. Seventeen. Do you read?"

The other Corpsman's radio came to life. "Twenty-two. Twenty-two. Is everything A-OK? We're picking up distress from your body readings. Is everything all right?"

Peter wiped sweat from his forehead. He stared at Twenty-two's radio. He went to one knee, picked it up, and found the correct button. "You won't be picking up any more body readings from your boys. They ran into a problem."

"Who is this?"

"Don't worry about that," Peter said. "You have a pretty good idea."

"You won't get away with this."

Peter bowed his head. He held the radio against his forehead. "Probably not, but I guarantee you, one way or another your Group isn't getting away with what it's done either. Either here or on the other side, you'll pay and so will The Group." He tossed the radio to the ground, ignoring the response from the other end.

Carrying Moses, Jack ran to the scene.

Way hurried to take Moses. He squeezed the baby to his chest. Moses squealed.

Jack studied the scene. "I heard the commotion. What's all the hullabaloo?"

Peter tilted his head toward Way. "Well, Way saved my life." He related the events to Jack.

"He saved your life as you was saving me and the boy's lives." Jack tugged at his cap. "I'll be switched. A lot of life saving going on."

Way heard something. He shielded his eyes against the rising sun and scanned the sky. "Listen."

"Choppers," Peter said. "We have to get back to Mom and get out of here."

Peter led the way back to the campsite, with Way, who carried Moses, on his heels. Jack had trouble keeping pace. Shamus stayed beside Jack.

"What is it?" Mom asked.

"They're coming again!" Peter called. "We have to go! Now!"

Four helicopters came into sight.

Peter grabbed Way. "You lead the way! Go!" He pushed Way in the back. "Follow him, Mom! Come on, Jack! Come on!"

Shamus barked.

Way took a few steps, then turned to see what was happening behind him.

Jack bent. Huffing. he leaned on his knees. "Go on. I'll just hold you back."

Peter grabbed Jack's shirt. "No way. You're coming, too." He started running almost dragging Jack.

A couple of helicopters landed at the campsite.

The other helicopters gave chase, passing over Peter and Jack and positioning above Way, Moses, and Mom. Corpsmen from each of them fired.

Way, carrying Moses, and Mom ran again. Way let Mom take the lead.

"Ah!" Mom lurched. She dragged her right foot several feet and fell. Blood soaked the back of her shirt and her pant leg and more came.

Way knelt beside Mom. "Mom!"

Peter and Jack caught up. Shamus bounded around them.

The helicopter flew ahead and made a turnaround.

Peter and Jack pulled Mom into the underbrush.

Corpsmen from the landed choppers called to each other.

"Leave me," Mom said. "I can't go anymore."

"No, Mom." Peter examined her back and thigh. His head dropped.

"They ... they got ... me, didn't they, Brother Peter?"

Peter took a deep breath. "I'm afraid so."

Jack muffled a sob. Shamus whimpered and nuzzled his snout against Mom's neck.

"You all ... go on. There ain't ... no more hope for me ... in this life." Mom coughed.

"Hang on." Peter cradled Mom's head in the crook of his arm.

"Ain't no use. Go. ... Thugs'll get you." Mom gave a feeble wave. "Go."

Peter sighed.

"Brother Peter?"

"Yes, Mom."

"I'm cold." Mom folded her arms across her chest and pulled them tight. "Do you ... think ... it's cold in Heaven? You know ... how I hate ... to be cold."

Peter chuckled. He held Mom tighter. He managed to smile through tears. "No, Mom. It's not cold in Heaven. It's just perfect."

Mom smiled. "Good." She closed her eyes. "You know how I hate to be cold."

"I know."

Mom took her last breath.

Peter lowered her head to the forest floor. He looked at the others. "I hate to leave her like this, but we have to go."

Jack stood straight, pulled off his cap, and held it over his heart. He gave a quick nod.

Helicopters flew in from every direction. There were at least ten of them.

There was the familiar sickening *whirr* of drones. They, too, came from every direction. There must have been at least a hundred.

Peter pointed deeper into the woods. "That way!"

Helicopters swirled above them, kicking up dust, leaves, and twigs. Drones whirred around them. In places where the woods were too thick for the helicopters to land, Corpsmen lowered ropes from them and slid to the ground.

Peter led the others, weaving between trees and brush.

Although they were outside, Way felt like walls closed in on him. He couldn't look any direction without seeing a helicopter, drone, or Corpsman.

As Way and the others ran into a clearing, several Corpsmen appeared in front of them. They turned left. More Corpsmen. They did an about-face. More Corpsmen. They turned right. More Corpsmen. There was nowhere to go.

Way held tighter to Moses.

Peter clutched his hair, closed his eyes, and exhaled.

Jack dropped to his knees. He pulled Shamus close.

"Make way," a Corpsman called. "Make way."

The Corpsmen in front of Way and the others parted. A Corpsman in a more decorated uniform, apparently an officer, walked between them.

The officer took off his helmet and sunglasses as he approached. His smile sent chills down Way's spine.

"Well, well, well," the officer looked Way up and down, "so this is the famous runaway." He snickered. "Oh, by the way, I'm from the government, and I'm here to help."

Drones by the dozens landed around the rebels and Corpsmen.

The officer put his helmet and sunglasses back on. He sauntered around Way, Peter, and Jack. He stopped in front of them. Looking at the younger Corpsman next to him, he ducked his head toward Way and Moses. "Get the offspring. Take him away."

"No!" Way clutched Moses tighter and turned away from the Corpsman. "No!"

The Corpsman grabbed Moses and tugged.

Peter and Jack jumped the Corpsman and pulled him away.

Corpsmen from all around descended on Peter and Jack and pulled them off their fellow Corpsman.

Shamus growled. He latched onto a Corpsman's forearm and wouldn't let go.

The Corpsmen threw Peter and Jack to the ground and kicked and hit them. One Corpsman pulled out a billy club and struck Peter on the head.

Another Corpsman clubbed Shamus. Two others grabbed Shamus and held him down. Another ran forward with a syringe and drove it into Shamus's neck. Bit by bit, the fight drained from Shamus until he gave a weak whimper and drifted into unconsciousness.

Other Corpsmen grabbed Way and yanked the wailing Moses from his grasp. One of the Corpsmen ran, carrying Moses, to a waiting helicopter.

Moses watched over the Corpsman's shoulder and reached toward Way. Red-faced and frantic, he screamed. "Da! Da!"

The Corpsman carrying Moses gave him to another Corpsman in the helicopter and climbed in. The helicopter ascended.

"No! No! Please!" Way crumpled to his knees. He covered his face.

Jack crawled to Shamus. Sobbing, he drove his face into Shamus's neck. Jack shuddered.

"Stand them up!" the officer barked.

Corpsmen did as they were ordered. They held Way, Peter, and Jack up and handcuffed their hands behind their backs.

Standing in front of Way, Peter, and Jack, the officer rocked from heel to toe. "This is going to be a nice little feather in my cap. You are looking at Brady Warsom, the officer who led the capture of the last runaway and the last rebels. Grand Matron Tannon is going to be very pleased with me." He stepped to Peter and held a finger under Peter's chin. "You have been a thorn in her side. You took the lives of some of the best people The Group had to offer."

Warsom stepped in front of Way. "And you, she is going to be particularly pleased to see you. The stunt you pulled, fleeing with an offspring who was set for extinguishment." He clicked his tongue. "Bad mistake. She is ready to make an example of you," he waved in Peter's and Jack's directions, "of all of you. By the time she's finished with you three, everyone in the World Community will know that one does not cross The Group. I'd love to be able to deal with you right now, swift and sure, but my orders are to take you back alive so your sentence can be carried out for all to see. One does not cross The Group."

"What happened to you?" Peter's mouth smacked from dryness.

Warsom furrowed his brow and slowly turned his head toward Peter. "Excuse me?"

Peter cleared his throat. "What happened to you? I figure you're about my age, would've been in your early teens when everything fell apart. Didn't you see it coming? Didn't your folks see it coming? How did you fall for it? Why did you fall for it?"

Head down, Warsom pressed a toe into the dirt as if squashing a bug. "Of course, my 'folks,' as you so quaintly call them, saw it coming. That's why I'm in this position now. They chose the right side. If you'll notice, I'm in a prime position here, and you're going to be tried, tortured, and executed in front of thousands of people who hate you and everything you stand for. On top of that, it will be broadcast for the viewing pleasure of billions of people in the World Community who, by the way, also hate you and everything you stand for."

"I hate to tell you this," Peter said, "but it's your parents who made the mistake. They didn't have the answer, and your Group doesn't have the answer, and your 'World Community,' as you so quaintly call it, doesn't have the answer."

Warsom punched Peter in the mouth. "Don't you speak ill of The Group or the World Community. The Group keeps order and balance in the world. Without it there would be chaos."

Peter licked the blood from his lips. He worked his jaw. "You know, even with all your wrongheaded beliefs, Jesus loves you," he set his feet and stood firm, "but I'm a little rough around the edges, and I'd like to wring your neck."

Warsom snorted. "Jesus." He spoke to the Corpsmen standing behind Way, Peter, and Jack. "Take them."

The Corpsmen pushed Way and the others along. Way noted Peter's manner. Despite the knot above his left eye and his bloody lip, he walked with his head high and his shoulders back, straight and strong.

Jack did the same. He did look over his shoulder at the unconscious Shamus and called to him. Shamus never responded.

The Corpsman behind Jack shoved him. "Get along, old man. The animal will be fine. The Grand Matron wants him to live out his life in the wild where he should be, not under the control, subjection, or oppression of another creature. He will be able to live his life the way it was meant to be."

Corpsmen shoved Way, Peter, and Jack into a helicopter.

The helicopter kicked up dust, leaves, and twigs as it rose.

Jack stared down at Shamus. "It don't look good, Pete."

"No, it don't, but if we just hang on, it'll be better than ever."

"How can you say that?" Way asked.

"I don't know everything about the other side of death," Peter said, "but I do know whatever's over there is better than anything this world ever had to offer."

Jack leaned his head back against the wall of the helicopter. "So you think this is it?"

"I'd say so." Peter raised a shoulder. "Death has always been sure, it's just that now it looks a little more sure than it used to."

Chapter 19—The Grand Matron

Grand Matron Filleen Tannon entered her regional office, followed by two armed Corpsmen. Her light brown hair was cut in a bob. She wore a gray jacket, a black blouse and a gray skirt. She went behind the mahogany desk and stood. She leaned forward on the desk. "So we have the runaway," she nodded toward Way and then toward Peter and Jack, "and the last two rebels."

One of the Corpsmen rolled the chair out from under the desk. Filleen sat. The Corpsman helped her roll the chair back into position. Filleen put her elbows on the desk and interlocked all her fingers, except the two index fingers, which were pressed together and pointed up.

Way's stomach turned. He thought he might throw up.

Filleen leaned forward and rested her chin at the tips of her index fingers. Although she was no higher than Way, Peter, and Jack she seemed to smile down on them. "Gentlemen, I run an orderly world. All The Group and I ask is that everyone follow the rules. The Group and I take care of everything. We ask nothing of world citizens other than that they fall in line, take care of their tasks, and obey. The Group takes care of everything for them. They have no worries. It's not hard. The last several weeks, though, you have brought a great deal of chaos to our well-ordered world. We don't like chaos. We like structure. Everyone knows the rules. Everyone follows the rules. Everyone does their part to be a good citizen of the World Community, and everything goes swimmingly." She gave a slight tilt of the head. "Mr. March, with what part of that did you have a problem?"

Way started to speak, but his voice caught. He cleared his throat. "Well, madam, my son, Moses, was set to be extinguished the next morning. My domestic partner wanted him extinguished, but I didn't."

Filleen narrowed her eyes. "Excuse me? Your what? Who?"

Way jerked his head back. He blinked. "My son. Moses."

Filleen leaned forward. Her chair squeaked. "I know you've been in the wilderness for several weeks, but surely you haven't forgotten, the offspring has no name until one is bestowed on him by The Group, and that does not happen unless the mother chooses to keep him beyond his first year. In this case, the mother's choice was to have the offspring extinguished."

"You can't do that!" Way bent forward and grabbed the arms of his chair.

The two Corpsmen each took a step toward Way.

Filleen closed her eyes. She took a deep breath and let it out slowly. "Mr. March, we'll have no more such outbursts. The Group fulfills the mother's wishes. Mother's choice. It's for the good of The Group, the World Community, the mother, and the offspring."

"What?" Way edged farther forward and gripped the chair tighter. "How is that for my son's good? What about what I want?"

Like two attack dogs on leashes, the Corpsmen both appeared ready to pounce if given the command.

Filleen looked from one Corpsman to the other, then to Way. "Mr. March, one more outburst and I will have no choice but to let these gentleman go about their jobs of protecting me. Now, let me explain from the top and most important. His extinguishment is for the good of The Group and the World Community because it eases the strain on resources. The Group has to constantly be aware of the world population and the use of resources. Can you imagine how many people there would be in the world if every mother chose to keep their offspring? And can you imagine what a strain that would be? The Group has many mouths to feed and many people for which to provide. If this offspring were allowed to live, he would take the food out of another's mouth. Do you want that?"

Way struggled for something to say.

Filleen continued. "I'm sure you don't. Now, for the mother's point of view and how the offspring's extinguishment is for her benefit. It will show how dedicated she is to The Group. She is putting the interests of the World Community before this offspring, who, again will be taking the food out of another's mouth if he lives. He will take resources that could go to another and so on. The Group likes to see its citizens put it above everything else. It will also help her in her task. She will no longer be cumbered with having to concern herself with this," she flared a nostril, "this, offspring. She will have a much better chance to rise through the ranks.

"I've had the opportunity to meet her and speak with her in the time since you made your mistake. She is an impressive young lady. I must say, your mistake proved to be what these gentlemen," Filleen motioned toward Peter and Jack, "and their misguided friends would call a blessing in disguise for her. Now that she's met me in person, it will definitely be a boost in her task life, and, trust me, she doesn't need an offspring weighing her down.

"And finally, how will this extinguishment benefit the offspring?" Filleen chuckled. "I'm glad you asked. Well, it will give him the chance to go on to Heaven," she gave a dismissive wave, "or wherever it is these people go. Maybe he can meet you at the pearly gates when you get there. Maybe he can sweep the streets of gold or some such nonsense." She rolled her eyes. "Really, for his good, this can keep him from suffering in life. Bad things may happen to him in this life. As great as The Group does in taking care of its people, occasionally pain or disappointment befalls them. This will save him from having to deal with that pain or disappointment, setbacks if you will."

"Lady, you are wackadoodle." Jack circled a finger around an ear. "A certified nut job. Kill him because he might have some problems in life? That's the craziest thing I ever heard. I knew dodos was extinct, but I guess loons ain't. Hmph. A certified nut job."

Filleen glared at Jack. "You do know your life is in my hands, don't you?"

Jack was leaned back in his chair, relaxed. He scoffed. "My life's in God's hands. Anything you got, you got because of him. He allowed it." He clicked his tongue. "You can do what you want with me, but I know where I'm going."

Filleen's jaw muscles tightened and loosened, tightened and loosened. "Are you going to join the offspring in sweeping the streets of gold?"

Jack guffawed and slapped his knee. "If that's my job up there, I'll do it in a heartbeat and be glad of it."

Filleen closed her eyes. She took in a measured breath. "I hope you know, sir, that within twenty-four hours you will be dead, and I'll still be here, doing fine."

"Twenty-four hours?" Jack slapped his knee again. "Glory be! Praise the Lord!" He hit Peter on the shoulder, almost knocking him out of his chair. "You hear that, Pete? Within twenty-four hours, I'm going to be in Heaven." He leaned forward. "And, lady, I don't care if I'm sweeping them streets of gold or dancing on 'em, I'm going to be full of joy just the same."

Way saw the blood rising from Filleen's neck to her face like the fires in the woods had climbed the trees.

Peter raised his eyebrows and chuckled.

The Corpsmen at Filleen's sides remained stiff and straight-faced.

Peter tugged at his ear lobe. "Ma'am, I'll tell you, I don't think you're going to get Jack down. The thing is, he's got too much to be up for."

Her face still red, Filleen moved her glare from Jack to Peter.

"You see," Peter said, "we know there's more than this stuff you see and feel and touch right here. I know you hate us and what we stand for, but let me tell you, there is a God and he loves you."

"Stop it," Filleen said through clenched teeth.

Peter tilted his head a bit. "No, please, let me go on. That God, the one true God, who loves you, sent his son, Jesus, to die for you, so you can spend eternity in Heaven, so you can have the same joy and peace Jack and I have now."

"Amen, brother," Jack chimed in.

Filleen's face grew more red. She narrowed her eyes. "I've heard it all. I've seen the videos of final interrogations before. I've attended thousands of punishments. Many of your kind have given the same tired, old spiel. I don't want to hear your fables and fairy tales."

"Now, ma'am, if you'd just consider the possibility," Peter said.

"The World Community has thousands of Christians, ministers, even, who say everyone will be all right," Filleen said, "that all faiths will go to your Heaven."

Peter dropped his gaze to the top of Filleen's desk, pursed his lips, and drew a breath. He lifted his eyes to look straight into Filleen's. "Thing is, ma'am, those folks are wrong. They're just as lost as if they'd never gone in a church or cracked open a Bible. Don't blame Jack or me or anyone else who believes the way we do. Jesus said it himself, there's no other way to the Father except through him. Anyone who tries to come any other way is a thief and a robber."

"Amen." Jack nodded.

Filleen sat straight. "I'm firm in my belief that all religions lead to the same place."

Peter held his thumb and forefinger a couple of centimeters apart. "You're that close. Actually, all religions but one lead the same place. That place is Hell, and the only one that doesn't lead there is Christianity. Of course, I'm including Jews who accept Jesus as the

Messiah in there, too. Any religion that doesn't center on Jesus Christ and him crucified is wrong. And there's only one of them that I know of."

Jack slapped his knee. "Amen, Pete. Man, you're preaching it up, brother and right here to the big kahuna, the tallest hog at the trough."

"As I said, I've heard it all." Filleen pressed a button on her desk.

Four Corpsmen entered the room.

Filleen motioned toward Peter and Jack, "Gentlemen, take these two men away. I'd like to speak to Mr. March alone."

As the Corpsmen led him away, Peter looked back over his shoulder to Way. "Remember everything we told you. Don't let her tell you any different."

One of the Corpsmen grabbed Peter by the shoulder and manhandled him through the doorway.

"We told you nothing but the truth, bud," Jack called back. "Hang onto it with everything you got."

Peter, Jack, and the Corpsmen escorting them were gone leaving Way, Filleen, and two Corpsmen in her office.

Way craned his neck, staring at the closed door behind him. He turned and let his neck sink into his shoulders. For the first time in weeks he didn't have Peter, Jack, Mom, or anyone else to lean on.

"Don't worry, Mr. March, you'll see them tomorrow." Filleen stroked her chin. "The vantage point depends on you. There will be an open seat next to me as I watch the final attempt to sway their beliefs. You can sit in that chair. Or you can be on the arena floor with them with thousands of people screaming for your head. Your choice. I'm sticking my neck out for you. The World Community wants you extinguished. The Group wants you extinguished. No one, including me, understands how you could have run away with the offspring the way you did. To commit such an act after all The Group has done for you, feeding you, clothing you, keeping a roof over your head. It's beyond comprehension. I'm willing to forget the whole thing. You have a chance to right your wrongs. All you have to do is publicly apologize to the mother, the World Community, and The Group and condemn the heinous acts of these men and those like them, speak out against their intolerance and their claims of knowing the only path to God." She shrugged. "That's all."

Way blinked.

Filleen sighed. "I know I've given you a lot to consider. Think about it, though. I'm giving you the opportunity to walk away from some of the most serious crimes that can be committed against The Group and the World Community: stealing an offspring that was marked for extinguishment, fleeing the city, consorting with rebels, being involved in the deaths of Corpsmen. The list could go on. But you, Mr. March, can just walk away. You could even be a help to The Group. You can witness to world citizens about the goodness of The Group in allowing you back into the fold after your transgressions. You can tell them about the evil and intolerance perpetrated by the rebels, the brainwashing attempts you had to endure. These are the last rebels. With your eyewitness account of what horrible people they are, you can help assure that no more rebels rise up and the World Community is safe from their kind from now on. What do you think?"

Way thought for several seconds; thought of his time in the woods with Peter and the others and all they did for him and Moses. "Actually, madam, they were good to Moses and me. They helped us survive."

Way was sure he saw Filleen's jaw tighten. There was more red to her cheeks.

"They helped you break the law," Filleen said. "It is obvious that if you choose to take me up on my magnanimous offer, you will have to go through a time of re-education. I'm afraid their brainwashing attempts were at least a bit successful. That's quite all right. Don't worry. It won't hurt a bit and before you know it, you'll be thinking clearly again."

"If I do as you say, can I keep my son? Can I keep Moses? When can I see him? I'd like to see him."

Filleen sighed. "'My,' 'my,' 'my.' The offspring doesn't belong to you. He belongs to The Group, to the World Community. You nor anyone else in the World Community own anything. The Group owns it all. Maybe we need to intensify our efforts. It concerns me that someone such as yourself can be raised in the care and nurture of The Group's teaching and after just a few weeks running in the wilderness with a bunch of savages all that teaching can be undone. All The Group's efforts appear to have been for naught. We must do better." She narrowed her eyes. "The Group's teaching was undone wasn't it, Mr. March?"

"I … I don't know. I don't think so. I mean, those people were good to Moses and me. They took us in, helped us."

"Did they sway your belief in The Group and its ways?"

Way rubbed his neck. "They …, well, they told me different things they think are wrong with The Group's teachings and beliefs. They told me about Jesus."

"Jesus." Filleen practically spit out the name. "A bunch of uneducated boobs told you about Jesus. If you want to learn about Jesus, The Group has scholar after scholar that can tell you everything you need to know. What did they tell you that was so great about their Jesus?"

Way studied his palms. "Like they told you earlier about him being the only way to get to Heaven. They said he loved me and died for me."

Filleen rolled her eyes. "Sure, Jesus loves you. Buddha loves his followers. Krishna loves his followers. It's all the same."

"I don't know. They made it sound different, special."

Filleen smiled and tilted her head. "All religions are special in their own way. The Group doesn't have a problem with religion, but they are all the same. The problem comes when people start claiming theirs is the only way." Her smile caused Way to shiver. "We all go along to get along. In the end, that's what The Group wants from all world citizens in all areas, not just religion or even lack thereof. We all do our part to help the world improve, to evolve. That's what matters. It's not the God you serve that matters, it's your contribution to the World Community. Are you a good world citizen? That's the question."

Way renewed his interest in his palms, rubbing them together. "I don't know."

Filleen leaned forward, her chair squeaked. "If you want to believe in Jesus, that's fine. It just can't be to the exclusion of the world's other great, and some not so great, religions. As wonderful as it all may sound to you, your beliefs hold not greater value than the Buddhist, the Muslim, the Hindu, the Mormon, or even the atheist."

"Actually, those aren't my beliefs. The people I was with, and they're good people, those are their beliefs. I'm still working on mine."

Filleen chuckled. "You and all world citizens should believe The Group's beliefs. Maybe you're the only one struggling with this, but I would have thought that someone who had been raised by The Group for almost twenty-five years would do better at withstanding a few weeks under the influence of those misguided individuals."

"They're persuasive."

"Be that as it may, they're also dead men. They are the last rebels. When they're gone, the World Community will be free of their exclusionary, judgmental, bigoted views. It will be a fresh start for personkind." Filleen took in a deep breath, exhaled, and stretched. "I can almost feel the shackles falling off right now, feel the freedom. How about you?"

"I don't know. I guess I'm not quite there yet."

Filleen rested her elbows on the desk. "You've been through quite a harrowing experience. Some would say a rampage, even. You kidnapped a child, went outside the city unauthorized, aided and abetted rebels, maybe even murdered some of the World Community's best and brightest. That's what you've done in The Group's eyes. Now, from your perspective, you endured several weeks of captivity and brainwashing."

"With all respect, ma'am, I wasn't held captive. I was free to come and go as I pleased. There were no chains, no bonds of any kind."

Filleen sat back. Her chair squeaked. She raised her interlocked fingers to her chin. "You might not want to say that too loudly." She spoke to the Corpsmen. "You gentleman can forget you heard that. Nothing, nothing that is said in this meeting leaves this room."

The Corpsmen nodded.

"Now," Filleen turned her attention back to Way, "there may not have been physical bonds," she poked a finger to her head, "but I can assure you, they worked on your mind and emotions. Those kind of people were not going to be satisfied with The Group's idea of everyone just getting along, 'You believe what you want, and I'll believe what I want.' They want everyone to convert to their way. Don't you see a problem with that?"

Way wiped sweat from his forehead. "I guess it's a problem, unless it's true."

Filleen sat straight, her eyes widened, eyebrows raised. "Really, now?"

"They told me things, showed me things from their Bible. A lot of it made sense. You know, came together."

Filleen tilted her head to one side. "So now you're a scholar? You're an expert on ancient, practically prehistoric writings? Look, Mr. March, I'm a Christian. I believe in Jesus. I do." She motioned toward the Corpsman standing beside her. "I would wager these gentlemen are Christians, but unlike your friends, none of us are so narrow-minded as to think we have a monopoly on truth."

"I don't know. All I know is what Peter and all of them told me. Now, about my son. If I accepted your proposal, would I be able to keep him?"

"He's not yours. Everything and everyone is part of the World Community. All of it belongs to The Group. On top of that, it would set a dangerous precedent. The mother chooses what to do with an offspring on the first anniversary of its birth. This mother chose to have this offspring extinguished, so, regretfully, I have to refuse your request. There is one bright spot on the horizon. If you choose to apologize to the World Community and return to society, as I understand it the domestic partnership you've been in for three years is over, maybe you can be matched with another partner who would be willing to birth an offspring, and maybe that partner would be willing to let said offspring go beyond its first anniversary. Something to consider."

Way's stomach rolled. His heart fluttered. "My son, Moses, has he been killed? Is he dead?"

Filleen curled her lip and flared a nostril. "Mr. March, that sounds so crass, so barbaric. I'm afraid you're development took several steps back in your time with those people. That's not good for the evolution of personkind. If you accept my offer, you will definitely need to go through a re-introduction into civilized society. But, to answer your question, yes the child has been ext—"

Way didn't hear anything else. He fell from the chair onto his knees and buried his face in his hands. "No!" he wailed. "No! How could you? Moses! Moses!" He crumpled to the floor and curled up in a ball. Tears dropped to the wooden floor.

After a couple of minutes, Filleen had the Corpsmen lift Way into his chair. He sat hunkered over, forearms on his thighs, and face still buried.

"Sit him up," Filleen said.

Each Corpsman grabbed a shoulder and pulled Way into an upright position.

"I can see this is traumatic for you," said a stone-faced Filleen. "I tell you what, I'll make your choice for you. I will let The Group know how horrific your time in the wilderness was and what those people did to your mind and emotions. You will get special attention and be re-introduced into society. It's obvious those people damaged you greatly. Your case will not be a failure. It will be a great success. You will be a shining example of The Group's greatness and what the World Community can accomplish when we all work together." She smiled. "Tomorrow, during the cleansing, there will be a seat beside me, and you will be in it. You will have the best view in the arena to see what The Group does to the last rebels, those who so cruelly wrecked you." She nodded to the Corpsmen. "Take him away. See that he is well fed and gets plenty of rest."

Chapter 20—The Cleansing

Way sat alone in the room Grand Matron Tannon provided him for the night. After the cleansing the next day, he would be moved to the re-education facility to be re-introduced into society.

He sat on the side of the cot, the only piece of furniture in the gray room. Other than that there was a picture of the Grand Matron on one wall, a speaker on another and cameras hanging in each corner.

Over and over, he replayed the day's conversation with the Grand Matron. He replayed the night he took Moses and ran from the city. He replayed his time with Peter and the others. He wondered what he could have done different to protect Moses. Moses. Mostly he thought of Moses.

If Way had not run, Moses would have been extinguished weeks ago. Luka would never have been convinced to do otherwise. At least running had given him more time with Moses; time in which he was encouraged to spend time with and play with the boy, instead of he and Moses being seen as nuisances the way Luka had seen them.

There was no window. Way had no idea what time it was until the speaker crackled to life. It was time for the Grand Matron's Encouragement. It was 10 p.m.

The recorded voice of Grand Matron Tannon came through the speaker. "I serve The Group. The Group knows best. The Group has my best interests in mind. It is all about The Group. I am nothing without The Group. The Group takes care of me. The Group loves me. The Group is all I need. The Group has all I need."

Over and over. Over and over. The recording would play until 6 a.m.

Way laid down and rested his head on the pillow that didn't amount to much more than a folded towel. He pulled the blanket over his head, turned to lay on his side and pulled his legs in tight.

The next morning, Way was awakened by someone entering his room.

A Corpsman carried a stainless-steel food tray and set it on the foot of the cot. "Here's breakfast. You have thirty minutes to get to the arena. The Grand Matron is waiting for you."

Way sat up. He blinked and rubbed his eyes.

With an open palm, the Corpsman pushed Way in the back of the head. "Hurry. I don't think we should waste World Community resources on you, but apparently the Grand Matron thinks otherwise. Personally, I think it's a shame to feed someone who turned his back on the civilized world and ran away to live with the rebels."

Way eyed the palm-sized splat of watery mush and the brown banana on the tray. "Doesn't look like they're wasting much on me."

"You shouldn't expect much after what you did. Eat."

The Corpsman hovered while Way forced himself to eat. A couple of times the food almost came back up, but Way held it in.

Way swirled his spoon around the glob.

"What? You think you're too good to eat World Community food now?"

Way flared a nostril. "I think anybody should be too good to eat this."

The Corpsman pointed at one of the cameras. "You better behave. The Grand Matron is probably watching you."

Still hunkered over the tray, Way peered at the Corpsman out of the corner of his eye. "Do you know what it's like to live without cameras watching you constantly?"

"Why would I even want to know that? It's for the good of The Group, the good of the World Community."

"Is it really for the good of the World Community? The good of private citizens, like you and me?"

"Of course. It enables The Group to make sure all of us stay faithful and loyal and that we all act in the best interests of the population at large."

"I believe you're just spewing out what's been drilled into you all your life. I had a chance to be away from the cameras. It was nice. I'm sure there were satellites that could watch us most, if not all, of the time I was out there with my friends, but you would be amazed how good it feels to be able to live without a camera staring you in the face all the time."

"You're crazy." The Corpsman snorted. "The Group needs to be aware of what world citizens are doing. The video allowed them to get a quicker start the night you escaped. The satellites helped them track you and your friends. They saved a lot of person-hours and resources."

"I'm afraid you're the one who's crazy." Way stirred his spoon around the glob. "One, you eat stuff like this, and two, you fall for everything The Group tells you." He motioned toward a wall. "When I was out there, I went to bed when I was tired, not when someone told me to. I ate when I was hungry, not when someone told me to. You have no idea."

"The rebels got in your mind. We need to be watched. We need taken care of. The Group loves us. The Group has everything I need. The Group takes care of me."

Way swiped the tray off the cot. It clanged on the concrete floor. The glob splattered. Way leaped from the bed and grabbed the Corpsman by the collar. "The Group has nothing! The Group stole your soul! It sucked the life out of you and everyone else! It doesn't care about you or anyone else! Can't you see? Can't you see?"

The door opened and three Corpsmen rushed in. They grabbed Way and wrestled him down, smashed his cheek to the floor, and held his hands behind his back. One of the Corpsmen slapped handcuffs on his wrists.

The Corpsman that had brought in his food, stepped on Way's back, pressing hard with his boot. "Now, our orders are to get you to the stadium for the refining. For some reason, the Grand Matron wants you beside her. If it wasn't for that, you'd be part of a refining in here right now. Another trick like that last one and we'll shoot you up with so much sedative you won't ever know again who you are or where you are. Take him."

The other three Corpsmen dragged Way out the door.

Filleen stood and offered a slick smile when a Corpsman led Way into her private box at World Community Stadium. "Mr. March, it's so good to see you. I'm afraid you're running late. We've delayed the refining just for you."

The Corpsman nodded with slight hesitation. "Apologies, Grand Matron, we had some trouble getting him around this morning."

Filleen put a light touch on the Corpsman's back. "No worries. We can let your tardiness pass this time. Mr. March's is an unusual circumstance."

"Thank you, madam." The Corpsman ducked back against the wall.

"Mr. March," Filleen clutched Way by an elbow, "as promised, I have a seat for you right here by me. We will enjoy the refining together."

She led Way to a chair that was just a couple of feet from the plate glass window.

Way stared out over the massive throng. Banners snapped in the breeze. Drones crisscrossed above the stadium. People cheered the World Community Orchestra as it played the World Community Anthem. The stadium's grass looked almost too green to be real. The sun shined bright.

On a raised platform in the middle of the field loomed the guillotine.

Way's throat tightened. Knots formed in his stomach. The glob from breakfast almost came up. His knees went weak. The guillotine seemed to be right there; Way felt like he could reach out and run his fingers along the blade.

Filleen directed him to his chair. "Sit here. I have to address the fine citizens."

Way sat. He didn't remember any other refining looking quite this festive.

Filleen stepped to the window. It slid open. A Corpsman gave her a microphone.

"Good citizens of the World Community, good morning."

The crowd roared.

Filleen waved. "Thank you all for joining us today, and thank you to all who are joining us via the World Community News Network. This is a record attendance for a refining. We also expect to have a record number of viewers."

Way scoffed. Everyone in the World Community was required to either attend refinings or watch them in some form, whether or not it was a record depended on if the population was up or down.

Filleen continued. "It is a record, but alas," she poked out her lower lip, "the hope is this will be the last refining."

The crowd groaned.

Filleen laughed. She pumped her fist in triumph. "It will be the last refining because today we relieve the World Community of the last rebels."

The orchestra struck up a celebratory tune. The crowd roared.

Filleen waited a few seconds then quieted the crowd. "Yes, these are the last rebels. After these two intolerant bigots are taken care of, The Group, Corpsmen, and the World Community at large will no longer have to deal with their kind. These men and others in their band have been brought to justice. After years and years of searching and using valuable World Community resources, I can now say that all rebels have been brought in. We call it a refining. It is the World Community that is being refined. The World Community will be better, purified, with the extinguishment of these intolerant ones. The rest of us will be allowed to move forward in the evolution of society, of personkind."

Spectators cheered.

Once again, after several seconds, Filleen quieted them. "Take note, World Community, after this morning's refining, we will no longer speak of them or their wrongheaded beliefs. We cannot risk seeds of rebellion being planted. To rid the World Community of that risk, The Group will no longer allow world citizens to speak of these men, their kind, or their value system. Any person or group that claims to hold the only true belief or the only true way will be dealt with quickly and harshly. Make no mistake, The Group and the World Community will not hold any one religion or belief system above another. They are all equal."

Cheers arose once more.

Way felt the knots in his stomach tighten. He shook as he wiped sweat from his forehead.

"World citizens are free," Filleen said. "You are free to believe as you wish, but you have to allow the other person to believe as they wish. Any intolerance will be met with rapid judgement." She paused then chuckled. "I know you are not gathered here to listen to me."

Way felt the crowd's excitement welling.

"So with that," Filleen said, gesturing toward a ramp at the north end of the field, "I give you the last rebels!"

Peter and Mountain Jack appeared in the entrance with Corpsmen following. Peter and Jack had cloth sacks over their heads. Their hands were bound behind their backs.

The crowd gave its loudest cheer up to that point. The stadium rocked. Way grasped the sides of his stadium seat. Spectators at field level pawed at Peter and Jack and spit on them.

The Corpsmen pushed Peter and Jack through the mass.

Jack tripped and tumbled hard to the ground, unable to break his fall. The Corpsman directly behind him bent among the people, out of Way's sight, and came back up, holding Jack by the shirt collar.

Way took a deep breath. His lip quivered. He tried to focus anywhere but the field.

Filleen squeezed Way's forearm. "Aren't you enjoying this? You don't seem to be. You used to love the refinings. I had my video coordinators find it. We have footage. You used to be one of the most enthusiastic ones at these events."

"I … I was wrong. That was wrong."

The crowd tore at the sacks over Peter's and Jack's heads, finally ripping them off. The Corpsmen continued to push Peter and Jack along. A spectator punched Jack in the jaw. Another hit Peter from behind at the base of the skull. Someone punched Peter in the stomach, doubling him over. A teenage girl slapped Jack. Another spectator kicked him from behind. An elderly man hit Peter in the head several times with a shoe.

Way didn't know if his friends would survive the walk to the platform. "Can't you stop this? Can't you get it over with?"

Filleen smiled. "Mr. March, this is the last time we get to do this. I need to let the people have their fun."

"But, Peter and Jack, they just wanted to live their lives and hold their beliefs." A tear rolled down Way's cheek.

"They took the lives of several Corpsmen. If they had their way, they would spread their message of intolerance. They had to be stopped, and they had to be made an example. We can't have anyone else taking up their cause. It must be stopped."

Way looked to the door. Five Corpsmen stood between him and it.

The window to the skybox was open. Way craned his neck to see how high he was above the lower level.

A Corpsman grabbed him by the shoulder and pressed down. "I wouldn't think about it. If the jump didn't kill you, the people down below would. You're not the most popular person in the World Community right now."

Way slumped back in his seat.

Peter and Jack neared the platform.

One of Peter's eyes was swollen shut. Streaks of blood ran down his face. His shirt was tattered.

Jack's nose and lips bled. Like Peter's, his shirt was tattered. He dragged his left leg.

The crowd loved it.

Filleen smiled and clapped. She squirmed in her seat and squealed. "This is wonderful!"

The Corpsmen around them mumbled their agreement.

"Isn't this wonderful?" Filleen gripped Way's forearm.

Way pulled away. He sunk further into his seat.

A Corpsman got in front of Peter and dragged him up the steps.

Another Corpsman pushed Jack up the steps, tripping him a couple of times.

The Corpsmen positioned Peter and Jack at the guillotine. They faced them toward Filleen's booth.

Filleen stood at the open window.

Way looked from Filleen to the open window. The best he could, he took a quick glimpse over the edge. *"What if …?"*

Again, the Corpsman at his side gripped his shoulder. "I wouldn't. That's the only thing that could make you more unpopular. She is the only one keeping you alive right now."

"Fellow citizens of the World Community," Filleen said, "again, I welcome you to this festive occasion. Today, we take a huge step forward in personkind's evolution. This is a refining; not for these men, they have been given ample opportunity to repent of their intolerant ways. This is a refining for the World Community. Today, we rid the world of the last rebels, the last ones standing in the way of personkind's growth and progress. These rebels standing before you today represent the end of all intolerance in the World Community."

Way lowered his head and closed his eyes.

The Corpsman grabbed Way by the hair and pulled his head up. "Watch. This will be good for you."

Filleen continued. "Their poison ends today."

The crowd cheered.

"With that," Filleen gave a slight nod, "I ask you to make way for the man who will do the World Community a great favor!"

The stadium rocked.

People pressed hard around the platform.

Corpsman parted the crowd from the north entrance all the way to the platform.

Way knew who was coming.

A man in a bright yellow suit ran into the stadium waving the World Community banner. He stood out against the grays of the crowd.

It was the deliverer.

Way had seen this man, or other deliverers at all the other refinings whether in person or watching on video. Other than the grand matron, or grand patron, whichever it happened to be at the time, he was the star of the show. The flair he put into the refining could make it special; at least that's how Way used to think. It was entirely different when two friends were on the platform awaiting their fates.

Way's chest tightened. Breath came hard. Sweat rolled down his forehead.

Chapter 21—The Deliverer's Show

The deliverer bounded up the platform steps and raced around the platform waving the banner. He stopped on the side of the platform closest to Filleen and placed the banner in a stand. He bent low and then stood tall, raising his arms, working the crowd up. He repeated. The crowd responded. He repeated. The crowd responded. Way had never heard the stadium so loud.

If Peter and Jack were the last rebels and this was truly the last refining, Way wondered what the deliverer's purpose would be from then on. Of course, he would be the toast of the World Community and could probably take his pick of tasks, especially if he made this show good enough. Judging by the crowd's enthusiastic response, he seemed to be well on his way to accomplishing that.

The deliverer blew kisses to the crowd. He took several deep bows. He pranced around the platform.

Way got sicker, thinking how he used to enjoy the refinings. Filleen was right. He used to be one of the most enthusiastic celebrants.

The deliverer went to Jack. He grabbed Jack's beard and lifted. He pulled a marker out of his pocket and drew a line across Jack's neck. The crowd loved it. The deliverer laughed and urged the crowd on.

Mountain Jack stood tall, at least a head taller than the deliverer. After what Way had seen of Jack in the woods, he wished Jack was free and could get ahold the deliverer. The deliverer wouldn't stand a chance, even though Jack had to be at least thirty years his senior.

The deliverer moved behind Jack, lifted a foot, and used it to push Jack toward the guillotine. Jack took a couple of steps. Again, the deliverer lifted a foot and pushed Jack in the backside.

Way grimaced. "When will this be over? How long is this going to last?"

Keeping her eyes on the field, Filleen smiled. "Why, Mr. March, you know once the head's off, the show's over. We have to build up to the euphoria."

"Please, can't you be decent and get it over?"

"I'm afraid the rebels have ruined you. Or at least tried to. No worries. With some intense rehabilitation, you will once again be a sterling world citizen. You will make The Group proud."

"I don't want to make The Group proud. I want my friends to stop suffering."

Filleen waved. "Be that as it may. What must take place, must take place."

The deliverer had Jack at the guillotine. Jack stood straight. He complied with what the deliverer wanted from him, didn't fight, beg, or plead.

The deliverer turned Jack and, with the help of a couple of Corpsmen, laid Jack on the bench and scooted him until his neck was in the blade's path.

Jack found Peter. "Come on in, boss man. The water's fine."

Microphones on the platform picked up his voice and carried it all over the stadium. And with that, all around the world.

Way shook his head. "Wow."

The deliverer scowled. He slapped Jack. He grabbed a banner and pranced around the platform, re-energizing the crowd. He stopped, gave the banner to a Corpsman, and faced Filleen's booth.

He held up both hands, fingers extended. With exaggerated movements, he started the countdown. "Ten. Nine. Eight. ..."

The crowd joined in.

Jack found Peter again. He smiled. "I'll catch you on the other side."

The deliverer moved in position to trigger the guillotine. "Five. Four. Three. Two. One!"

The deliver released the blade. The guillotine did its job.

Peter fell to his knees.

The crowd erupted.

Way lowered his head.

The deliverer took several deep bows.

Holding the microphone, Filleen approached the window. "Thank you. Thank you. We are down to the last rebel. The leader. For years, this man led rebel attacks against The Group."

Way knit his brow. His jaw dropped. "He did no such thing," he said to no one in particular. "He, all of them, just wanted to live in peace and be left alone."

"Shut up," a Corpsman said. "Listen to the grand matron."

"For years, decades even, this man and others like him have terrorized the World Community. No more. After today, their message of hate and intolerance will be silenced forever."

Just when Way thought the crowd could not get louder, the decibel level increased.

After several seconds, Filleen motioned for the crowd to quiet. "Deliverer, I turn this man to you. Do what you must." She returned to her seat.

Laughing, the deliverer raised both arms. The crowd roared.

Like Jack before him, Peter stood tall, shoulders back.

"Wait! Wait!" A Corpsman raced through the north entrance and across the field and charged up the steps to the platform.

He leaned on his knees, catching his breath. Finally, he motioned the deliverer over.

The deliverer went to the Corpsman. The Corpsman whispered something to him.

Eyes wide, the deliverer broke into a huge smile. He danced on his tiptoes and lightly clapped.

The deliverer moved to center stage and faced Filleen's suite. "Madam Grand Matron, I have a surprise for you."

Filleen shivered and danced in her seat. "Oooh, I love surprises." She went to the window. "What would that be, sir?"

The deliverer paced around Peter. "It has just come to my attention that in the time from when this rebel was ten to twelve years old, he dislocated his right shoulder three times while participating in some forms of competition. Might I add, that is another great argument for The Group banning such barbarous activities. Be that as it may, it makes this portion of the refining more interesting."

The deliverer moved behind Peter and grabbed his wrists. He pulled back.

Peter leaned forward to his tiptoes. The deliverer kept lifting. Peter grimaced, but didn't cry out.

Way winced. "Jesus, please help him."

Filleen shot him a look. "What was that?"

Eyes ahead watching the torture, Way hesitated. After a few seconds, he took a breath. "I said, 'Jesus, please help him.'"

"That's what I thought. Let me remind you, your re-education is going to be difficult enough for you. Quite intense, in fact. Don't do anything to make it worse."

Way kept his eyes forward.

The deliverer let go of Peter. Peter took several deep breaths.

The deliverer stretched Peter's arm straight out to the side. The deliverer massaged Peter's shoulder. He leaned close to Peter's ear. "The right shoulder, eh?"

The deliverer grabbed Peter's right wrist.

In Filleen's suite, Way winced.

The deliverer yanked.

Peter's knees buckled a bit, but he didn't go down.

Spectators cheered.

Running his fingers up to Peter's shoulder, the deliverer clicked his tongue. "Hmm, not quite there." The deliverer circled Peter. He stopped in front of Peter and turned to the crowd. "What do you think, dear people?" He held out his hands, tipping them like scales. "Should I leave it at that," the scales went up and down, "or should I finish this little part of the refining?"

"Finish it!" called a voice from a corner of the stadium.

"Finish it!" called a voice from another part of the stadium.

A voice here.

A voice there.

More voices here.

More voices there.

"Finish it! Finish it! Finish it!" They chanted and stomped. Stomped and chanted. "Finish it! Finish it!"

"Finish it," Filleen whispered. "Finish it."

The deliverer took hold of Peter's outstretched arm. "You heard them, rebel," he cooed. "It's what the people what. I can't go against the will of the people." His voice rose. "And they said, 'Finish it!'" With that he yanked.

The deliverer's headset picked up the sickening *pop* and carried the sound for all to hear.

Way grimaced.

Spectators roared.

Peter's knees buckled, but he managed to right himself without falling. He folded his right arm at his chest.

"Well, well, well." The deliverer sauntered around Peter. "So, rebel, how does that feel?

Peter stood straight, eyes closed.

The deliverer kicked Peter's backside. "I said, 'How does that feel?'"

Peter managed to keep his balance.

Moving in front of Peter, the deliverer wrenched his arm to the side. "Let me fix that for you!"

Peter bent at the knees, but still didn't go down. Grunting, he lifted his face to the sky.

The deliverer gripped Peter's wrist and worked his way up to Peter's shoulder. "Tsk. Tsk. Poor rebel. Your shoulder is still out of place. Well, I'm sorry. I've done all I can. It looks like we have to move on."

The deliverer punched Peter in the stomach. Peter doubled over.

The deliverer waved, working the crowd. He went to a table on the platform and picked up a club. He stood behind Peter, took a comically exaggerated corkscrew wind-up and swung, hitting Peter across the backs of his knees.

Peter buckled and went down to his knees. He lifted one knee and got a solid foothold. He stood.

The deliverer acted impressed, then took his stance again. Another exaggerated wind-up and another blow behind Peter's knees. Peter went down.

This time it took a little longer, but Peter lifted a knee, got a foothold and stood. He wobbled.

The deliverer stopped. He eyed Peter's feet. He took his stance and hit Peter behind the knees.

Peter went down.

Way closed his eyes. "Stay down, Peter. Stay down."

After a several seconds, Peter lifted a knee, got a foothold and stood.

The crowd "oohed" and "aahed."

Peter swayed like a tree blowing in a breeze.

The deliverer fumed. He threw down the club, grabbed Peter's hair and pulled him to the guillotine.

Filleen squirmed. "Here we go."

Way closed his eyes. "No. No. No," he said under his breath.

A Corpsman nudged Way's shoulder. "Pay attention."

Filleen let her attention drift from the platform to Way. "Yes, do. It's important that you see this."

The deliverer positioned Peter on the guillotine. He turned and gestured, inciting the crowd.

"The last rebel," Filleen said. "To think, this is the last one."

"Lord, please forgive them," Peter called loud enough for the deliverer's microphone to pick up.

"Fool." Filleen sneered.

Peter looked toward the booth where Way sat.

Way wasn't sure if Peter knew he was there. Way stood. A Corpsman grabbed Way's shoulder, but Way pulled away and stepped to the window. He waved, hoping Peter would see.

The deliverer started the countdown.

Peter nodded. "Way, remember, Jesus loves you and died for you!"

Forehead and palms pressed against the window, Way watched. "Jesus loves me and died for me."

"Three! Two! One!"

The deliverer triggered the guillotine.

Way lowered his head. His fingers slid down the glass.

The deliverer went to each side of the platform, receiving the spectators' adulation.

Filleen clapped. "Well done! Well done! Those were the best ever!" She moved to Way's back and clasped his shoulder. "Now that we're through all this, we can get you back to being a productive world citizen."

Way pulled away from her grip. "No! I won't! You can't make me. You can do what you want to me," he put a finger to his temple, "but you can never take away what's in here." He pointed to the platform. "Jack and Peter and everyone like them, they had something worth living for and worth dying for. Your Group has nothing worth either."

Filleen grasped Way's wrist. "Mr. March, you're going mad. We want to help. The Group wants to help. I want to help."

"Get away!" Way stepped back. "When you killed my son and my friends, you took away every reason I had to live." He squared himself. "I choose Jesus. I choose the Jesus Peter and Jack chose."

Filleen closed her eyes and put her fingers to her chin. She turned to a Corpsman. "Open the window. Get the deliverer's attention. Don't let anyone leave. We'll see how serious Mr. March is. We'll scare this nonsense out of him." She pointed at two Corpsmen then Way. "Get him."

The Corpsmen grabbed Way.

Holding the microphone, the Corpsman that Filleen sent to the window did as he was told. "Uh, deliverer, stop. Everyone, s-stop. No one is to leave. We have … there's a …"

Filleen moved to the window. She grabbed the mic. "Give me that, fool." She smoothed her blouse and skirt. "World citizens, hear me. It seems I was wrong."

The crowd gasped.

Filleen smiled. "Yes, hard to believe, I know. But, it is to your benefit. It seems those intolerants that I thought were the last rebels, were not."

The people murmured.

"We have another rebel in our midst." Filleen motioned for the Corpsmen to bring Way to her. She pulled Way close. "This man, the runaway, who The Group was so graciously willing to forgive says he wants the same fate as those rebels."

The crowd went for it in the same manner Way had seen Shamus go for meat after a hard day in the woods.

Filleen nodded. "I know. I know. It's almost too good to be true." She turned to the Corpsmen. "Take him."

The Corpsmen took Way out of the booth and onto the concourse. There weren't many people there, mostly Corpsmen and other officials.

It was different when they got off the elevator at the lowest level. From the second the doors opened, the battle ensued. Corpsmen pushed Way. The crowd grabbed at him, scratched him, spit on him, pulled his hair, tore his clothes, punched him, kicked him.

Way almost fell, but caught himself. He figured if he went to the ground, it was over, he wouldn't have to worry about the guillotine.

They reached the platform. A Corpsman pushed Way up the steps. The deliverer reached and met him halfway, grabbing his shirt and pulling him up.

Way fell to all fours. The deliverer kicked him in the seat of the pants, and Way fell prostrate.

"See, he's in submission to The Group!" the deliverer crowed.

Way struggled to all fours. "Jesus, please help me."

The deliverer kicked him in the seat again. Way was ready and held firm. He raised, resting on his knees.

Way looked to the sky. "Jesus, please forgive me for sinning, for all those years that I was blind, for believing in The Group."

The deliverer grabbed the back of Way's shirt and held a mic to Way's mouth. "What are you muttering, rebel?" He pulled the mic away. "Oh, wait, no one cares."

The crowd laughed.

The deliverer marched around the platform. "The last of the last rebels! Get it well in your heads, world citizens, none of you want the same end that is about to befall the runaway. This is what happens when you turn from The Group. This is what happens when you stray from the path. Neither Grand Matron Tannon nor The Group want us to have to do this again. ... But they will authorize it again if necessary. And again ... and again ... and again. With this refining, The Group will wipe out the last vestige of the false teachers of these so-called followers of Jesus. We all know they've taken the words of that great teacher and distorted them. The Jesus we know would not be pleased with their bigotry and hate."

Way bent forward, his forehead touching the platform and his palms to his face. "Thank you, Jesus, for your forgiveness. I believe you are the Son of God. You are the only way."

"The runaway mutters again. Ignore him. He's misguided, delusional."

The deliverer yanked Way to the guillotine. Two Corpsmen positioned him and tied his wrists and feet.

The deliverer knelt beside Way's head. "You have one more chance. Will you accept The Group's gracious forgiveness? Will you rejoin the World Community as a useful citizen?"

Way swallowed hard. His mouth was dry. The blade towered over him. "Never. I choose Jesus."

The deliverer's jaw dropped. "You do realize what's about to happen, don't you? You do know once I trip the switch there's no stopping that blade, right?"

"I know, but it doesn't matter. There's nothing here for me. My place is with Jesus."

The deliverer huffed. He straightened and walked the platform. "Let the runaway's fate be a lesson to all. You must guard your mind. The Group knows best. The Group has your best interests in mind. It is all about The Group. You are nothing without The Group. The Group takes care of you. The Group loves you. The Group is all you need. The Group has all you need."

"Not true!" Way struggled against his bonds. "Not true! The Group controls you! The Group sucks the life out of you!"

The deliverer ran to Way and covered his mouth. He looked to a Corpsman. "Gag him."

The deliverer turned Way over to the Corpsman. He resumed walking the platform. "Let me remind you of the grand matron's words. She said it about our previous rebels. I'm sure now it extends to the runaway. Once this is over, he is never to be spoken of again. His kind is never to be spoken of again. Their vile teachings are never to be spoken of again. The runaway and his kind bring division. We want unity. We are one world. We are one community." He smiled. "We are the World Community. Let's be done with the runaway!"

The crowd went into a frenzy.

The deliverer pumped an arm over his head. "Ten! Nine!"

The crowd joined in.

Head turned to one side; Way caught sight of a teenage girl who was not counting down. She looked from one side to the other, apparently making sure no one was watching. She held her palms together at her chin, like Way used to see Mom pray, and glanced upward. "I'll see you there." she mouthed, pointing to the sky.

Way nodded. He closed his eyes. The crowd noise was muffled.

"Three! Two! One!"

There was Jesus.

Way fell to his knees. "Praise you! Praise you! Praise you!"

Jesus smiled, took hold of Way, and urged him to stand. He pulled Way into a hug. Jesus released Way. He stepped back. "Welcome home."

Way had never felt anything like he felt at that time. He knew there were no more worries. No more problems. There was joy, peace, lightness.

Way hopped back and forth. He laughed and danced.

"Hot dog! I knew you'd make it!"

"Mountain Jack?"

Jack shook Way's hand. "You got it! It's me and better than ever!"

Way looked Jack over from head to toe. "But—"

Jack looked down at himself. He clutched his stomach. "Different, ain't I? Don't have quite the gut you knowed me with.

This coming to Heaven deal is the best weight loss plan ever." He laughed. "Me and Pete get you in a ballgame now and we'd thump you good with me not having all that extra baggage to carry. It's like I lost a whole person." He flapped his elbows and danced from side to side. "I'm more spry, too." He stopped and poked Way in the chest. "I figure I must be about your age now." He cackled and danced a circle. "And I'm going to stay that way forever! Whooppee!"

"Hello, there, young man!"

Way turned to see Mom approaching.

Like everyone else Way saw, she appeared to be around twenty-five to thirty years old.

"I thought you'd come around," Mom said. She touched Way's cheek. "So good to see you, boy. So good to see you." She turned and motioned toward a man following her. "I'd like to introduce you to Donald. He was my husband in my life on the old earth."

Donald nodded. "Nice to meet you, son. Good to have you with us."

"And, of course, you remember my boy, Abe."

Way couldn't help himself. He grabbed Abe in a bear hug, which Abe returned. "You sacrificed your life for me. I wouldn't be here if it wasn't for you."

Abe stepped back. "Ah, it's what Jesus did for all of us. It was just the right thing to do. It was the least I could do after I was such a jerk to you."

"Hey, bud." Someone from behind grabbed Way's shoulder. He turned. "Allen?"

Allen nodded. "You got it."

"Hey, are you all having a reunion without me?" Peter approached, followed by three women. He hugged Way. "It's good to see you." He stepped back and swept an arm out in a half-circle. "Isn't this great? Isn't it even better than we told you?"

Way took in the scenery: greener grass than he'd ever seen, a bluer sky than he had ever seen. Peace, joy, and love so strong he could almost touch them. "It …, it …, I can't even describe how beautiful it is or how I feel. Wow."

"Amen." Peter motioned the women forward. "Way, this is my wife, Sandi, or at least she was my wife on earth, and my two daughters, Elaine and Rene. And, again, at least, they were my daughters on earth."

Sandi smiled. "Nice to meet you."

Way took her hand. "Nice to meet you, too," he nodded toward Elaine and Rene, "all of you. Peter's a big reason I'm here. Well, all of these folks are. I'm thankful God had them find me in the woods. I don't know what would have happened to me."

Jesus stepped in. "There are some others who want to speak to you."

Three men and three women stood to the side, smiling.

Way gasped and pointed at one woman and one man. "You were my parents!"

"Yes, we were," Way's father said. "I'm Edward, she's Teresa."

The three of them hugged.

Way stepped back, but still gripped Teresa's shoulder. "But, how ... what are you doing here?"

"We didn't become Christians until after The Group took over," Edward said. "We'd heard about Jesus before, but didn't believe. Both of us had heard of Jesus, of the gospel, but hadn't responded. When we saw the direction the world was going and started searching the Bible, it all made sense."

"By the grace of God," Teresa said, "we started that search before they took the Bibles away from the common people."

Edward nodded. "True. We became Christians and served Jesus in secret for a couple of years. You came along and eventually reached the age that The Group was going to take you away and raise you the way it wanted."

Teresa pressed her fingers together at her chin. "We couldn't let that happen. We knew you'd be brainwashed like they were doing everyone else. We prayed so hard for you."

Edward held Teresa close. "That we did. Under the circumstances, we didn't receive a lot of teaching, but we knew to pray, and we prayed the best we knew how."

"It just came to, we refused to turn you over to The Group," Teresa said, "and The Group wouldn't have that. That was an offense punishable by death."

"You mean you died the same way I did?" Way said.

"Yes, they did," Jesus said, "and for much the same reason, too. They had true parental love for you, just as you had for your son. There are more who want to speak to you." He motioned to the two men and two women who stood to the side.

They stepped forward.

"We're your grandparents," said one of the men. "I'm Albert, your father's father, and this is his mother, Frances." He gestured to the other man and woman. "Here we have your mother's parents, Gary and Joan."

Way huffed. "Amazing" He rubbed his head.

Albert nodded. "Yes, it is amazing. God is amazing. All of us prayed for you before you were born. Actually, before your parents were even born."

"Yes, before your parents were even born," Joan said.

Way noticed some of his own mannerisms in each of his grandparents: a tilt of the head, a smile, a gesture. "Prayed what?"

Gary had a twinkle in his eyes. "Mostly that you'd live for the Lord and end up here."

The other grandparents agreed.

"I don't know that I really lived for him."

"In the end, you did," Gary said. "You certainly died for him, and you did end up here."

Way took in the unspeakable beauty. He grinned from ear to ear. "Yes, I did, didn't I?"

"In addition to praying for you, we prayed for your children and your further descendants," Frances said. There was not a grandmotherly wrinkle to be seen. "We didn't know how long things would go on, so we prayed for the whole family line."

"You prayed for my children?" Way came to a realization. "Moses? Where is Moses? What did The Group do to him?"

"I'm here," came a voice from behind the crowd that had gathered to watch the reunion. Moses stepped out.

Way bounded to Moses and gave him a hug tighter than any except the one he gave Jesus. They swung back and forth.

After releasing Moses, Way studied him up and down. "They killed you?"

Jesus nodded. "Yes, they did. His mother carried on with her plan to have him killed."

"Best thing that ever happened to me." Moses laughed.

"I'd say." Way beamed. "It's so good to see you!"

"Good to see you, too." Moses's smile lit up his face.

Way put an arm around Moses. "We missed out on a lot because of the way things were, but I think we'll make up for it here."

Smiling, Jesus gripped each of them by a shoulder. "No doubt about it."

ONLY THE BEGINNING

www.ingramcontent.com/pod-product-compliance
Lightning Source LLC
Chambersburg PA
CBHW071330120626
46546CB00002B/508

* 9 7 8 1 9 6 0 3 2 6 6 1 4 *